Water for a starving world

*This revised version of the original Swedish edition
is published in cooperation with the United Nations/UNESCO
as part of the information component of the United Nations
Water Conference.*

MALIN FALKENMARK
GUNNAR LINDH

Water
for a starving world

Translated by Roger G. Tanner
Foreword by Yahia Abdel Mageed
Preface by Ven Te Chow

WESTVIEW PRESS
BOULDER, COLORADO

Swedish edition published in 1975 by Natur och Kultur, Stockholm

Published 1976 in the United States by Westview Press, Inc. 1898 Flatiron Court Boulder, Colorado 80301 Frederick A. Praeger, Publisher and Editorial Director

Library of Congress Cataloging in Publication Data

Falkenmark, Malin, 1925-
  Water for a starving world.

  Translation of Vatten at en svältande varld.
  "In cooperation with the United Nations and UNESCO, and in conjunction with the United Nations Water Conference."
  Bibliography: p.
  1. Water-supply. I. Lindh, Gunnar, joint author. II. Title.
TD345.F1913   363.6'1   76-45475
ISBN 0-89158-211-8 (hardcover)   ISBN   0-89158-212-6 (paper)

Printed and bound in the United States of America

CONTENTS

FOREWORD

Malin Falkenmark and Gunnar Lindh have done a great
service to the world community in calling attention to the
overriding importance of tackling the world's fresh water
supply immediately, effectively, and on a broad scale. Their
book *Water for a Starving World*, which first appeared in
Swedish and is now being made available to a wider,
English-speaking public, strikes a fine balance between the
experts' concern for accuracy of detail and the general
public's need to be informed about this all-important matter
in terms which ordinary citizens can understand.

Our thanks are due to the United Nations Educational and
Cultural Organization (UNESCO), which saw the need and
arranged for the translation of the work.

The truth is that the world is faced with a water crisis of
staggering dimensions. The fact that the total water available in the world is probably sufficient to meet all our needs
begs the question. To be usable, the water must flow where it
is needed, in quantities sufficient for the task, and be of a
quality that meets reasonable health and similar requirements.

To cite just one example: there are few great cities in the
world today that are not likely to face serious and costly
water supply problems in the years ahead. Population
growth, the surge of the rural population to the urban
centers, industrialization with its use of water as a coolant,
and pollution caused by the carrying off of effluents and
debris have placed strains on water supply systems under
which they cannot for long stand up. A great deal of work
will have to be done to improve municipal water supplies.

One of the most immediately urgent water needs is for
agriculture, where vast population increases must take place
if world food targets are to be met. Much of this new
requirement must come from water savings effected by the
elimination of outmoded and wasteful methods of water use.

The United Nations Water Conference, which will be held in Mar del Plata, Argentina, in March of 1977, and which most of the United Nations' 145 member nations plan to attend, will review these problems and suggest solutions to them. Some of the solutions will be technological, more of them will call on managerial skills, and all will have to have political backing and commitment if they are to succeed. Nor will action at the national governmental level be enough. Increasingly, the initiative for new works to be undertaken will have to come from communities and small groups of citizens working together to meet a common need. It is our hope that the conference will not only be effective in promoting cooperation between countries (for example, in the management of international river basins), but will also help to mobilize the support of the general public for the far-reaching programs which must be undertaken internationally, nationally, regionally, and in cities, towns, and communities, down to the smallest hamlet.

That is why a work such as *Water For A Starving World*, with its emphasis on communication between scientists and policymakers, administrators and technicians, experts and members of the public, is of such great importance to the task in which we are all engaged. I hope it finds the widest possible readership.

Yahia Abdel Mageed
Secretary-General
United Nations Water Conference

PREFACE TO THE
ENGLISH-LANGUAGE EDITION

Water is the most abundant natural resource on earth. Essential to most human activities, it can mean life or death, bounty or poverty, war or peace. Some areas are blessed with generous supplies of water, but face the threat of destructive floods. In other areas, water is often all too scarce and there are deadly droughts. It takes forty liters of water to produce one can of vegetables; yet in some regions of the world there often isn't enough water for any plant to grow. Fresh water is indispensable to crops and meat, to irrigation, to inland fisheries, to forests that protect land from erosion and supply building and other useful materials, to public health, to housekeeping, and to recreational and numerous other uses. The entire human civilization hinges on sufficient water supplies for its sustenance and progress.

Water is commonly taken for granted as nature's gift. Not only are there wasteful usages, but industry and people pollute and poison available water supplies at a frightening rate. If there is to be enough available fresh water when and where it is needed, the costs of purification and delivery are going to be very high. In fact, the supply of water is by no means unlimited. The lack of water, rather than of land, may become the principal constraint on efforts to expand world food output and to keep world peace.

Water problems are centuries old, and problems of industrial pollution date back to the beginning of the industrial revolution. Increasing abuse of water resources together with expanding population and industry have greatly multiplied the problems and their seriousness on a worldwide basis. Unless there is international cooperation as well as national coordination in the search for remedies, trouble lies ahead for many countries and for the world.

In the atmosphere of this urgency, a series of water-related world conferences have been organized. First, there was the Water for Peace Conference sponsored by the United States in Washington, D.C., in 1967 to call attention to the need for international cooperation in water resources development as essential for world peace. Five years later, the United Nations Conference on the Human Environment, in Stockholm, was held to consider a wide range of water-policy problems. Water was then recognized as a critical element in world development activities. There was also much discussion of water supplies and management problems in 1974 at the UN World Population Conference in Bucharest and at the UN World Food Conference in Rome.

Now in the planning stages is the UN World Water Conference to be held in Mar del Plata, Argentina, in March 1977. The conference will consider how the global fixed stock of water can best be managed to satisfy the world's mounting requirements for water for domestic, agricultural, and industrial uses. Its principal objective is to promote the awareness and the actions needed locally, nationally, regionally, and internationally if a water crisis is to be avoided within the next few decades.

The International Water Resources Association, a nongovernmental organization, concentrates on promoting water resources development for the benefit of mankind. The association's First World Congress on Water Resources was held in Chicago in 1973 and focused on "Water for the Human Environment." Its Second World Congress, with the theme "Water for Human Needs," took place in New Delhi in 1975. In preparation is its Third World Congress, which has adopted the theme "Water for the Human Survival," to be held June 2-7, 1978, in São Paulo, Brasil. The aim of these congresses is mainly to provide an international forum for developing interdisciplinary communication and international understanding in the field of water resources, with a hope that future water crises can be alleviated.

Governmental and nongovernmental organizations' activities, however, are limited. Attendance at their conferences and participation in their activities are largely confined to delegations and members. In order to broaden the scope of achieving their objectives, other effective media must be sought. Publication of information that will reach the general public is an efficient method; but while many books have been written on water, very few provide an adequate exposé of the current critical situation of world water problems. In fact, until now, there have been none written for the layman who is essentially the very pillar of our society and world.

Water for a Starving World was written by two outstanding experts who are actively engaged in water sciences and technology, but who communicate easily in nontechnical terms. The book was originally written in Swedish and published only a year ago. At the invitation of the United Nations, it has now been translated into English. Publication of this English-language edition is not only timely in that it heralds the forthcoming UN World Water Conference, but is also most welcome as a grand service to mankind: it alerts the public to the worldwide critical water problems that we face today and that we hope to solve in this and the next generation.

Ven Te Chow
President
International Water Resources Association
October 1976

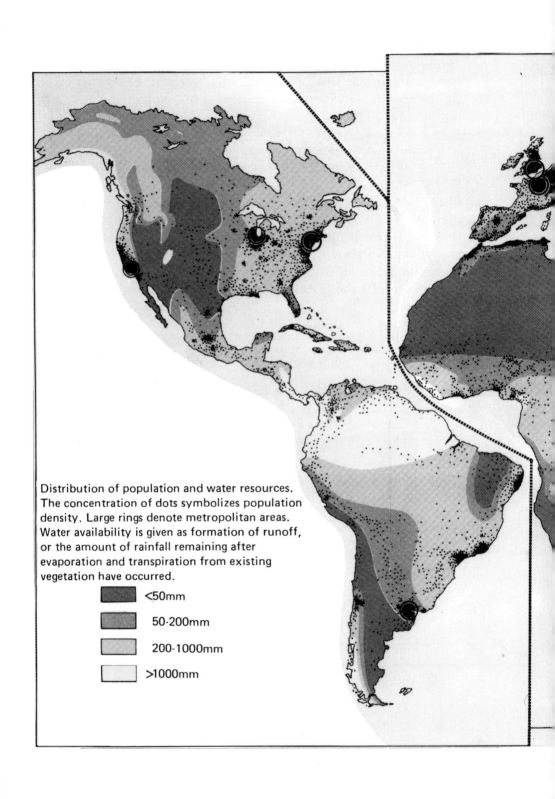

Distribution of population and water resources.
The concentration of dots symbolizes population
density. Large rings denote metropolitan areas.
Water availability is given as formation of runoff,
or the amount of rainfall remaining after
evaporation and transpiration from existing
vegetation have occurred.

<50mm

50-200mm

200-1000mm

>1000mm

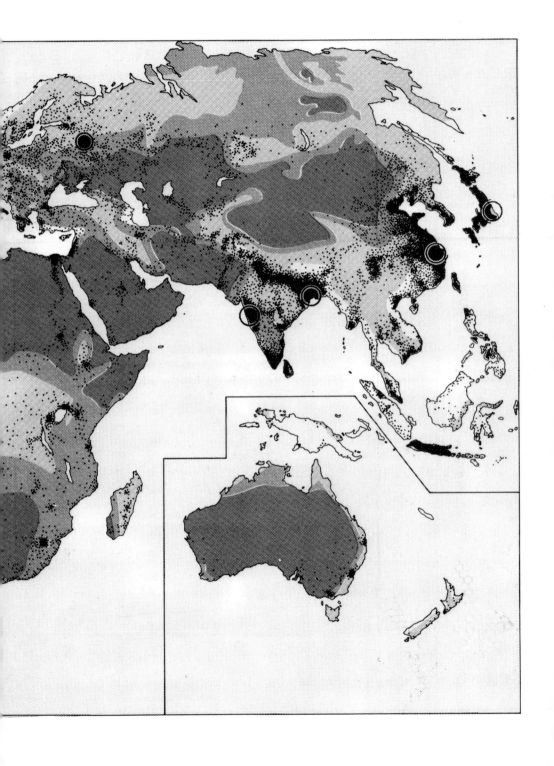

1   *Introduction*

Disaster has already struck

Hundreds of millions of people in the world today are starving in the sense that they are chronically hungry and have no chance of leading the normal life which is widely regarded as a human right. According to the most conservative estimate, there are already 460 million starving people, but the figure is constantly rising. A great many of these people live in the countryside; they are smallholders, tenant farmers, or unemployed and landless laborers. The ranks of the hungry also include the slum populations of the cities.

The numbers of starving people are increasing all the time. According to the plans for increased agricultural output, drawn up within the United Nations (UN) Food and Agriculture Organization (FAO) early in the 1960s, output should have risen by an average of 3.5 percent per annum during the past ten years. The actual rate of increase has been slower, amounting to no more than 2.6 percent per annum. In other words, production has barely kept pace with the growth of population. Starvation has not been relieved. Instead, the numbers of the hungry have increased during this period.

The global crisis of food supply which now faces us has been brought about by a combination of several factors. The excessively slow rise in the production of food for a steadily growing world population has been accentuated by a number of temporary setbacks. During the early 1970s, adverse weather conditions simultaneously affected many regions in different parts of the world. This is an unusual occurrence. The USSR, China, India, Australia, the Sahelian zone along the southern edge of the Sahara, and Southeast Asia were all affected in this way, so that in 1972 the total world production of grain fell for the first time in over twenty years. Compared with the previous year, production fell by 33 million tons instead of rising, as planned, by 22 million. This led to a severe shortage. Since then, the shortage has been aggravated, first by a shortage of artificial fertilizers and then by a rise in oil prices and the rapid inflation which followed in its wake.

The ten-year forecasts of development which were compiled for the UN World Food Conference held in Rome during November 1974 indicate that the situation will have greatly deteriorated before 1985 unless food production is radically improved, above all in the developing countries.

If the total grain shortage were to be remedied through imports of grain by the countries affected, this would place an impossible burden on world trade. The developing countries must, therefore, be helped to step up their own food production, and measures are urgently needed not only to make agricultural output more reliable but to improve crop yields. Since the majority of developing countries are situated in the dry zone, *water is a key factor* in securing and improving their food production.

Water-surplus and water-deficiency areas

If we look around the world to find where there is a surplus of water and where there is a deficiency, it becomes apparent that the developing countries are far more at the mercy of their water supplies than are many of the industrialized countries. In the map on page 3, water supply from precipitation is compared with the water requirements of plant life. Hydrologists refer to the latter as potential evaporation. In simple terms, this corresponds to the water loss from a well-cared-for lawn with an ample supply of water. Put another way, potential evaporation results from the water requirements of vegetation when it is governed by climatic conditions alone.

The map shows that many of the developing countries are situated in water-deficient zones. It is therefore easy to

2

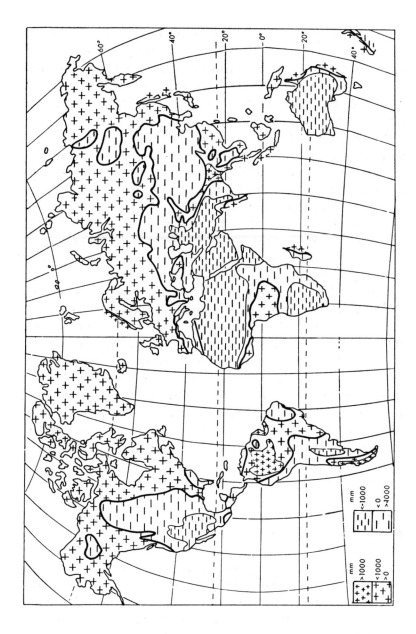

Water-deficiency (-) and water-surplus (+) zones in the world. A water deficiency exists if precipitation supplies less water than would be needed for well-watered vegetation. In the reverse circumstances there is a water surplus.

understand that agricultural conditions in most developing countries are very dependent on the compensation of this water deficiency. In its natural state, vegetation in these regions suffers from a shortage of water, at least during certain parts of the year when the air is warm enough for cultivation to be possible.

The map also shows that there is a water surplus in the tropical areas of the equatorial zone, where precipitation is so copious that a great deal of water is left over when the needs of vegetation have been supplied. These are the areas of the tropical rain forests. The cultivation problem here is posed by the surplus rain, which has the effect of leaching cultivated land. For this reason, fields can be cropped only for a few years at a time before being taken out of cultivation.

Comparing this map with a map of original vegetation, one finds that the natural type of vegetation is very clearly governed by the existence of a surplus or deficiency of water. Vegetation in the deficiency zones takes the form of steppe, prairie, or savannah when there is a moderate shortage. A greater deficiency gives rise to desert or semidesert. In India, which is predominantly situated in the water-deficiency zone, the vegetation is monsoon rain forest, the reason being that vegetation of this kind can survive on less water than a well-tended lawn. The vegetation of surplus zones is decidu-ous or coniferous forest in temperate climates, and tropical rain forest in the tropics.

The water factor is vitally important to the agriculture of developing countries

As will be shown in greater detail in chapter 3, the water factor is of fundamental importance to long-term develop-ment and short-term fluctuation of agricultural output. This is particularly true of the developing countries, most of which are situated in zones where water supply varies a great deal both geographically and over periods of time. In those countries the year is often divided into a wet season and a dry season. In the arid zones, precipitation can vary a great deal

4

from year to year, and droughts are liable to occur for several years in succession. In developing countries which border on mountain areas, floods are common and add to the difficulties.

The water question will therefore have to be solved if the agricultural output of the developing countries is to be improved. Irrigation is one important ingredient of development, and drainage is another. The documents of the 1974 food conference in Rome make it clear that the slow rate of development during the past ten years can be ascribed largely to a failure to extend irrigation facilities on schedule or a failure to maintain the facilities which already exist.

Thus, one of the many causes of the failure of the Green Revolution—as has been observed, for instance, by Georg Borgstrom—is that no provision was made for the water factor. Fertilizers and high-yield varieties (HYVs) are useless without water in the ground.

The importance of water is also underscored by the fact that the thirty-eight poorest countries in the world are all situated in areas bordering regions of either snow or desert. Their poverty is characterized by inundations resulting from heavy meltwater floods or by a shortage of water.

Although the vast importance of the water factor to both urban and rural development is widely recognized, this factor has not generally been given the attention appropriate to its importance in the countries concerned. The entire range of problems has been woefully neglected, and this is part of the reason for the excessively slow rise in production.

The problem of water quality has been examined

The observation that the water factor has been neglected may possibly come as a surprise to the reader, particularly as there has been almost a surfeit of writings about water in the past few years. But the overwhelming majority of these writings has been concerned with the composition and purity (or impurity) of water—the quality of water, in other words. On the other hand, the quantity and flow of water have received

5

little attention until quite recently. The reason is that the problems of pollution are a living reality to us. They are more or less brought home to us, and they demand immediate action. Quantitatively, we are generally well supplied with water in the industrialized countries. The different state of affairs which can exist in a developing country in this respect has not really left any mark on the discussion of matters concerning development. This is probably the reason why no clear attempt has yet been made to put water supply into a total perspective.

For example, the question of water supply was seriously neglected when population development was discussed at the UN World Population Conference in Bucharest in August 1974. This neglect went so far that an estimate of the population which the world was capable of supporting was drawn up without any attempt to consider whether or not this population would have enough water! Again, the work which has been done within the global model of the Club of Rome has not included any discussion of the limiting role of water in general development. Water is treated as a technical facility only. In the first model, the only natural resources to be taken into account are the nonrenewable ones. In the second model, water is viewed merely as part of the agrotechnology which is assumed to be available. In the epilogue, however, it is observed that on a more long-term basis water demand will impose an external limit on development, above all through the medium of irrigation requirements.

The problems of water supply are upon us

The quantities of water used by man for water supply and irrigation are still quite small in relation to the total magnitude of water resources, but developments are moving fast, and the percentage of total water resources required for the maintenance of human society is rising steeply. It has been estimated that by the year 2000 the world's population will need to withdraw a gross volume of water corresponding to

6

nearly 25 percent of the total resource. This may not sound like very much, but the term "resource" refers to long-term annual averages. River runoff varies considerably throughout the year. Most of the water flows during short flood periods, while during the driest part of the year, the runoff is considerably below the annual average. Normally the flow which is available in the rivers amounts to between 25 and 35 percent of these annual averages.

Before the end of this century, we may reach a total water demand which—seen as a world average—approaches the minimum-season runoff in the rivers. One can, therefore, readily appreciate that we are rapidly heading for a period when we will have every reason to consider the role and the importance of water in development.

The problems of the developing countries concern all of us

The problems of the developing countries concern all of us. The Swedish people are already heavily committed, as witness the events of 1974 when, prior to the Riksdag debate on international assistance in December 1974, a massive body of opinion was organized in favor of the year's wheat surplus being used to form a reserve supply for disaster relief. Since the question of water supply is such an important key to an understanding of the possible development of the poorer countries, and since this question has been and still remains a neglected one, we have set out in this book to give a more detailed description of the role of water in development. Water problems in different parts of the world will be illustrated with particular emphasis on the problems of the starving continents. We wish to show what tools will be needed and what can be done to bring the world's water under human control. We will also show that there is enough water to go around, but only provided that we can manage it in such a way that it is used effectively and with proper regard for the problems of ecology.

7

2　　Population development and water

Water supports life and vegetation

Without water there could be no life on our planet. We can survive for quite a long time without food, as dieters and hunger-marching idealists have shown. But we cannot live for long if we are completely without water. Lack of water has sealed the fate of many a desert traveler: in the heat of the desert, man can survive for only a few days unless water is supplied to replace his body losses. Dieters and hunger marchers also must take care to supply their bodies with water; otherwise their efforts are doomed to failure. To take another example, we know that when small children have gastric influenza, it is very important to replace the liquid they lose; otherwise, convulsions and other complications are liable to occur.

Our society cannot function without water. Imagine what would happen if all the taps in a city suddenly ran dry. Cooking, domestic hygiene, and hospital services would cease, factories would have to close, and the entire machinery of society would disintegrate. City dwellers are extremely vulnerable in this respect.

Water is equally vital to agriculture and to rural households. Farmers have a difficult time in dry summers when wells run dry and water has to be distributed by tanker. Everybody in Sweden remembers the trouble and inconvenience that resulted from the prolonged spring drought of 1974.

All the tankers in the world cannot provide sufficient water for irrigation in a situation of this kind. Vast quantities of water are needed merely to supply, say, 20 mm to a field of one hectare: 20 mm on one hectare is 200 m^3 of water, and a tanker can carry only a few cubic meters. A quantity of 200 m³ of water would last a family of five several years. Each individual needs an intake of no more than about 3 liters per day in addition to water for dishwashing, hygiene, and laundry. In the developing countries, 25 liters per person per day, i.e., 125 liters per day for a family of five, is usually enough. Thus, one cubic meter is enough for eight days, and 200 m³ of water, the amount we need to irrigate one hectare of land, would last the family of five for more than four years! Irrigation uses very large amounts of water.

The essential importance of water is, of course, due to its being the central motive factor in all ecological contexts. Water carries nourishment to the cell and carries waste products away from the cell. Water is also the overwhelmingly predominant constituent of all living material. Every human being is made up of 60 - 70 percent water; the actual percentage varies somewhat between children and adults, men and women, fat people and thin people. Many foodstuffs contain more than 90 percent water. Cucumbers, for instance, contain a larger proportion of water than equivalent volumes of seawater. Seawater, with a salt content of 3.6 percent, contains 36 g of salts per kg, while the solid content of cucumbers is even lower.

The central role of water is due to the inner structure of the water molecule

The absolutely vital role of water in society is connected with its very special physical properties, which in turn are due to the internal structure of the water molecule. The two hydrogen atoms are fastened to the common oxygen atom in such a way that the water molecule has a surplus positive electric charge at one end and a predominantly negative charge at the other.

Because of this, water molecules tend to join together at low temperatures, the positive end of one molecule attracting the negative ends of its neighbors. This hydrogen bonding forms the water complex, or polymer. Normally, poly-

9

mers disperse their molecules at higher temperatures, because the molecules agitate more rapidly and pull at the molecular bonds; conversely, as temperature drops the bonds become tighter. Usually, then, substances get heavier, or denser, the colder they become. This is true for water down to 4°C, its point of maximum density, but below this point the hydrogen bonds, which were able to "twist together" in the liquid state, begin to stretch the molecules apart in the rigid, crystalline state. This reduction in density continues through 0°C, the freezing point of water, and so explains why ice is lighter than water. This quality is the reverse of that applying to other substances, which are heavier as solids than as liquids.

This too is the property from which water derives its high surface tension: the water molecules hold on to each other. The uneven charge also enables the water molecule to penetrate other charged substances. It is capable of parting the positive and negative constituents of salt molecules, and this is the property which makes water such an excellent solvent.

The water molecule also tends to adhere to different materials, such as soil and glass. This, together with its surface tension, enables water to rise through narrow tubes and cling to soil particles. Water is retained in the upper stratum of the soil, and it is from this soil water that plants derive the overwhelming proportion of their nourishment. Only plants with long roots are normally capable of extracting groundwater.

The mutual attraction of water molecules contributes to various other extreme properties. For instance, water has extremely high boiling and freezing points when compared as a chemical substance (hydrogen oxide) with oxides of the various relatives of hydrogen in the periodic system. If the normal rules of chemistry were to apply, water would freeze at -100°C and boil at -92°C. Water also has a very high heat-storage capacity, a property which is utilized in domestic heating systems and industrial cooling systems.

The Nordic countries owe a special debt of gratitude to the unique heat-storage capacity of water, without which the

10

climate of their latitudes would resemble that of Siberia. The Nordic countries receive a considerable amount of heat from southern latitudes by way of the Gulf Stream and wind humidity. The winds carry large quantities of heat which have been added to the water during evaporation in sunny subtropical latitudes and released in the atmosphere above the Nordic countries when the water vapor blown from the south is precipitated in the form of drops of water, or condensation. No less than 30 percent of the solar energy reaching the earth is absorbed in the hydrological cycle, which redistributes it around the world.

In certain cases water has to be transferred

How much water does our human society need? Before answering this question we must consider more closely what the water is to be used for. We can distinguish between two ways of using water. One is to use water *in the place where it occurs naturally.* For instance, in the production of hydro-electric power, water on its way down-river is made to drive a turbine, which in turn drives a generator and produces electricity. The fisherman also utilizes water in its natural location by catching the fish produced there. When we go bathing or boating, we visit lakes or rivers. We also utilize the tendency of water to flow from high to low levels. This enables water to carry things, and we make use of the river water to carry off waste products which we discharge into it. In agriculture and forestry, also, we make use of water in its natural location—in the ground in these cases. When the natural water supply is sufficient for our plant production, we say that our agriculture and forestry are rain-fed. If the natural water supply is insufficient, we have to resort to irrigation.

Irrigation implies that we have to *transfer the water,* diverting it from its natural course in rivers or underground. To supply our towns and cities with water, we extract raw water from a surface or underground source, purify it in a waterworks, and convey it through tunnels and conduits to the domestic water supply system, from which it is drawn as required through taps to kitchen sinks, baths, washing machines, and toilets. From there the water runs into sewers, which converge to form progressively larger tunnels carrying the water to a sewage treatment plant, from which the water is discharged back into a lake or river. The cycle is thus completed, and the water returns to the natural system. Irrigation water has to be collected in a similar manner. It is led off from a lake, river, or withdrawn from an aquifer (i.e., from a groundwater source) and collected in a storage tank of some kind before being channeled into the fields. Some of this water returns to the atmosphere by transpiration of plants and evaporation from canals and dams. A very small proportion is absorbed by the growing plants; the remainder percolates down through the soil and either becomes groundwater or is led off through drainage ditches to a river or stream. Thus, in the case of irrigation water the closing of the circle is a slightly more complex process.

Borrowed water must always be returned

Many of society's fundamental needs call for the diversion of water from its natural cycle. The water has to be "borrowed" for a time before it finally makes its way back to the watercourse in the form of sewage or drainage water. Sometimes it is returned to another "link" in the water cycle, as we saw in the case of irrigation, where some of the water is returned to the atmosphere.

One often meets the term "water consumption," but strictly speaking this term is only applicable in a technical sense, because "consumed" water never disappears from the global circulation system. The water simply moves from one place to another, and the most it can do is to change phase. Some of the water may evaporate, in which case it returns to the atmosphere. Some of it may be incorporated into manufactured products, but it is released sooner or later when the products are degraded. The remainder returns in the form of sewage or drainage water to the river or underground water-bearing formation to which it is channeled. Therefore, the diversion of water for the purposes mentioned above is no more than a shunting operation, a short-circuiting of the natural water cycle at one point or another. The water is deviated from its natural path, but after a time it will be back in the natural cycle again.

How much water can be borrowed in total?

In this chapter we shall try to view the development of world population in relation to the water resources on which that population is dependent to maintain its communities, industry, and agriculture. To start with, let us see how much water is really available.

In popular descriptions of water in the natural environment, one often reads that 94 percent of all water is contained in the seas, 4 percent is composed of inaccessibly deep groundwater, and 1.5 percent is frozen in the form of polar ice and glaciers. A mere 0.5 percent of all the water in the world is available to man.

But what does this really tell us? Nothing, really, because we are not concerned with the total volume of water in different forms. After all, we cannot empty the lakes, draw off all the groundwater and desalinate all the seawater. What we need to know is how much water we have at our disposal every day, month, or year and how much water we can extract without lowering our lakes and water tables. We therefore need to know how fast the water flows in its natural cycle. How much new water is added to watercourses and groundwater each year? Since every individual needs a certain quantity of water every year, the interesting matter is the annual flow which we all have to share. Clearly, then, *actual water resources are constituted, not by the volume of water, but by the speed at which that volume is replenished.* Water is continuously leaving a lake through an outlet, but at the same time, water is added to the lake through the inlet. We cannot drain the lake for our water supply. We can extract the new water supplied to the lake, but no more;

otherwise the lake would run dry.

The same applies to the groundwater reservoir beneath us. If we extract more water than is supplied to the reservoir by rainwater percolating down through the soil, the water table will sink. This has happened in many parts of the world, e.g., in the Colorado Basin. But the balance will be preserved as long as we do not take more than is added.

We can now understand that the earth's population is dependent for its supply of water on the *total flow of water circulating in the water cycle*. Together, the sun, sea, and atmosphere can be said to form nature's own gigantic desalinization plant and distribution system. The sun supplies energy and drives the "water wheel," so that fresh water is kept in circulation all the time—from the sea to the atmosphere, from the atmosphere to the land, and from the land back to the sea. This is the process known as the *hydrological cycle* or the *water cycle* (see figure below).

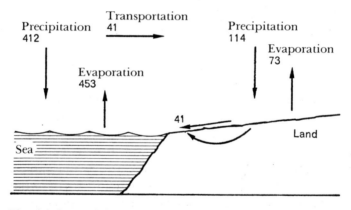

The global water balance (units of 1,000 km³ per annum).

In its natural state, fresh water is constantly on the move, and no water disappears entirely. Exactly the same water is circulating today as in the days of Cleopatra. This is something to be borne in mind when we turn up our noses at what is termed the reuse of water, for there is, in fact, no water on earth that is not reused.

14

Nature's own gigantic desalinization plant

Every year the heat of the sun lifts about 453,000 km³ of water out of the sea by evaporation. A more manageable unit of measurement in this context is the flow unit. One flow unit equals 1,000 km³ per annum. Seawater evaporation, then, corresponds to 453 units. Of these, 412 return to the sea in the form of rain. The remaining 41 units are carried by the winds over land areas, where they join the 73 units which have evaporated from the land areas. Altogether, 114 units are precipitated as rain or snow over the land areas and penetrate the soil to different degrees. Most of the precipitation returns to the atmosphere from water surfaces or damp soil surfaces, or as a result of plant transpiration. The remaining 41 units return to the sea again via rivers and groundwater flow, thus completing the water cycle. Excluding the ice and water which runs off in Greenland and the Antarctic, this leaves us with about 38 units in the inhabited continents. This is all that is available for water supply.

These 38 units, however, are an average for the whole of the year. Both precipitation and evaporation vary from time to time, with the result that river runoff too is often subject to distinct seasonal variations. At certain seasons of the year flooding occurs from spring thaw or rainy season, while during other seasons there is a low water flow in the rivers. In some regions, rivers dry up for parts of the year.

Variations in river flow are not as extreme as variations in precipitation, because the water is temporarily stored on its way back to the sea, e.g., in lakes, snow covers, soil, and in the ground. The larger the natural reservoir, the greater the equalization of river flow.

Variations in runoff during the year are more extreme in some parts of the world than others, owing to climatic differences and differences in storage conditions, e.g., many or few lakes, deep or shallow soil strata, etc. The average low-water flow for all continents is equal to approximately 35 percent of annual runoff. Thus, only about one-third of annual runoff is stable in the sense that it can always be counted on for any part of an average year. Putting it another way, total low-water runoff can be said to equal about 14,000 km³ per annum, or 14 flow units.

The remaining 65 percent of total river runoff—the difference between the total runoff of 38 units and the retained portion of 14 units, which is about 25 units—flows in the rivers for a short time in the form of spring floods or heavy rain floods. Floodwater, which is only available for short periods, disappears too quickly to be usable for purposes of water supply. It flows directly into the sea. Floods of this kind are in fact a disadvantage, because of the damage they cause, e.g., the recent disastrous floods in Bangladesh.

Water resources vary in different parts of the world

So far, we have considered the world as if it were a single, large unit. In fact, climatic conditions and geology vary considerably, with the result that hydrological conditions differ from one part of the world to another. The following table shows water resources in different parts of the world according to a recent estimate by the Russian scientist Lvovich. Geographically, however, this table follows the divisions observed by the UN in its work on population development prior to the Bucharest Conference, so that resources and needs can be directly related to one another. For this reason, some of Lvovich's figures have had to be converted.

It is not feasible to use more than 70 percent of the 38 units

How large a proportion of our total water supply can we count on being able to use? We can hardly drain our rivers of all their water. Consequently we dare not extract the whole of the stable portion of river flow, which, as we have seen, corresponds to 14 units.

One factor which increases the usable portion is that

16

Potential water resources in different parts of the world (mainly after Lvovich)

Continent	Runoff, km³ per annum			Stable runoff as percentage of total runoff
	total	stable portion*	unstable portion	
Africa	4 225	1 905	2 320	45
Asia, except USSR	9 544	2 900	6 644	30
Australia	1 965	495	1 470	25
Europe, except USSR	2 362	1 020	1 342	43
North America	5 960	2 380	3 580	40
South America	10 380	3 900	6 480	38
USSR	4 384	1 410	2 974	32
All continents, except polar areas	38 820	14 010	24 810	36

*Derived from groundwater, regulated by lakes or reservoirs.

people generally live all the way along a river valley, so that water has to be extracted at several points. The simple approach adopted earlier would hold good in reality only if everybody lived in one place. In fact, the same river water can be used several times over on its way from the source to the sea. If, for the sake of simplicity, we assume that we extract one-fifth of the low-water flow at ten different points along the river, the total extraction will be 10 x 1/5. In this way, an amount equal to twice the low-water flow can be extracted without extracting at any single point more than 20 percent of the actual quantity of water in the river.

The available water resources can be increased by retaining floodwater behind dams for use during subsequent low-water periods. This is done in the rivers of northern Sweden, where the spring flood is held in lake storage ready to be drawn off during the following winter when electricity demand is high but natural runoff is small. Storage measures of this kind are an essential precaution in areas subject to inundation.

Let us suppose that it were possible to build enough large reservoirs to capture all flood water, i.e., all the 25 units which run into the sea without having been used. Stable runoff would then be as great as mean annual runoff. In this way the entire annual variation would be limited, and 100 percent of the annual runoff would be available for use all the year round.

It is usually assumed that up to 10 percent of total water resources can be utilized without more than local difficulties, and that between 10 and 20 percent can be utilized given thorough planning of water supply. When the 20 percent mark is reached, however, water is considered to impose a limit on social development. (Further to this point, see page 34.)

Israel is probably the country where the greatest progress has been made in utilizing natural supplies of water. Water utilization there equals approximately 70 percent of resources, taken as an average for several years, but this requires advanced technology and continuous computerized accounting of all water flows in order to keep water utilization under constant surveillance.

Returning to our original question, what is the total amount of water which can conceivably be extracted for human use in the future? If the rest of the world were to develop the same efficient technology as Israel, this would give something of a maximum limit to real water resources. In this case 70 percent of the total resources of 38 units could be utilized. In other words, a maximum of 27 units would be available for water supply and irrigation. The main problems to be overcome are that the water may be present in the wrong place, it may be available at the wrong time, and it may not be of the right quality (i.e., it may be polluted).

Mean per capita water supply is rapidly decreasing

At present, about 10,000 cubic meters of water are available per person per year (m^3/person/year). This *per capita re-*

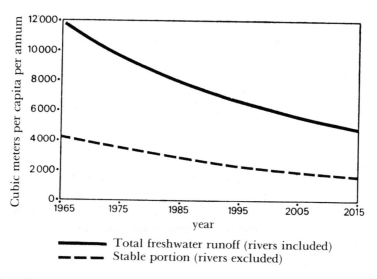

	Total freshwater runoff (rivers included)
- - -	Stable portion (rivers excluded)

Runoff in rivers and groundwater together constitute the water resources on which we depend for our water supply and for irrigation. The amount of water available per capita decreases with the growth of population. A certain proportion of the water flow is available all year round (the stable part). The remainder is only available during the high-water periods (the flood part).

source declines at the same rate as population rises. Given the population forecast for the year 2000, in 25 years' time the available resources will have fallen to just over 6,000 m³/person/year.

It is hard to envisage this amount. Let us compare it with the water requirement of individuals. This requirement is destined to increase as the living standards of the developing countries are expanded. Irrigation will be essential in order to guarantee sufficient food production. In round figures it seems reasonable to assume—as will subsequently be shown in more detail—that water requirements will rise to something in the region of 1,000-1,400 m³/person/year. This corresponds to about 20 percent of the average per capita amount which will be available in the year 2000. The above diagram gives some idea of the growth of the total pressure on total water resources.

19

Water is severely neglected in global discussions

It is interesting—and dismaying—to note that many of the experts who venture to draw up forecasts for the future, although realizing that water is a particularly vital commodity, nonetheless fail to calculate the water demand which their forecasts imply. It is perhaps arguable that the pressure on water supplies is really of minor importance, because other social factors will produce an untenable situation long before we reach the high population figures of the forecasts. On the other hand, this omission is highly unsatisfactory. The need for a widespread increase in water supplies should be taken into account *immediately,* not only because the total intervention in the water cycle will be extensive, but because it will take a long time and cost a great deal of money to organize the water supply which is a *necessary precondition for alleviation of hunger in our world.*

As mentioned earlier, water requirements were not analyzed before the UN World Population Conference in Bucharest. An estimate was made of the potential population the world was capable of supporting, and yet no investigation was made to see if there would be enough water! It became the task of the Swedish delegation to draw attention to this elementary requirement. Prior to the UN Food Conference in Rome, a debate was conducted in the mass media on the subjects of multinational corporations and alleviation of the immediate problem of world starvation. In Sweden, at least, nobody was told that water also constituted a problem, and nothing was said concerning the cost of the irrigation which will have to be provided *during the next ten years* to prevent world famine becoming several times more serious than it presently is.

How can people be so blind? Is it because those of us who come from industrialized countries, like some experts associated with agencies, are so used to having enough water that we simply cannot imagine a situation in which there is a shortage of water? In developing countries one of the principal everyday occupations of the womenfolk is to walk long distances to fetch water for their families. An enterprising villager can make a living out of the possession of a tap or a well. People in developing countries talk about water in the same way that we talk about the weather. And when the rains fail and the wells dry up, the real disaster is not far off.

An estimate of the future demand for water

Water supply, like climatic conditions, varies from one part of the world to another. There is a similar variation in the need to extract water, because irrigation requirements also vary with climate. We shall now consider how water supply and water requirements are related to one another in different parts of the world. The table on page 17 showed the total *supply* of water in different parts of the world. It also showed that the stable part of water supply, i.e., that portion which is available in the rivers all the year round, is relatively large in Africa and Europe and least in Australia, South and East Asia, and the USSR.

How great is the total *water need* likely to be in the future? How much water will be needed within the foreseeable future for public needs, for industry, and for irrigation? Let us make a conservative estimate, i.e., an estimate based on needs which are as low as they can be. We know that the cost of water rises quickly when more than, say, 10 percent of the available supply has to be used. A great deal of the cost of water is connected with the purification which is required before waste water is returned for reuse. The more water needed for water supply, the greater the amounts of waste water produced. If 10 percent of the water is extracted in a river and returned in the form of waste water, it will, on average, form a 1-in-10 solution with the 90 percent of the water remaining in the river. This is quite a concentrated solution. Pour a deciliter of dirty water into a liter of pure water and see for yourself!

It is our duty to ensure that not all the river water in the world becomes polluted. Because water demand is going to rise quickly, the rivers of the world will very soon be polluted unless we adopt a completely new philosophy of water use incorporating strict requirements for the purification of all water returned to watercourses. The more water to be extracted the more it will have to be purified. This will force a reduction in water requirements of our societies to a minimum.

To be realistic, therefore, we have to consider *what water requirements are truly fundamental* in the sense that water cannot be replaced by any other medium, such as compressed air, conveyor belts, etc.

Quite clearly, water is indispensable in the following instances for:

1. domestic use and for livestock, but only up to a level corresponding to a reasonable standard of hygiene;
2. industry, insofar as water cannot be dispensed with by the adoption of an alternative technology, e.g., in cases where water is now used to flush away various waste products; and
3. irrigation, facilitating the necessary production of foodstuffs, but also for the cultivation of industrial crops, e.g., vegetable seeds such as cotton.

How much water is needed for urban and rural supply?

As far as the population is concerned, the basic water requirement comprises the water needed for drinking and cooking, which is about three liters per capita per day.

In developed parts of the world, heavy individual use of water is often regarded as indicating a high standard of living. This may well be, but only up to a certain limit where all important needs have been provided for. We can set the limit at about 400 liters per capita per day, which is the amount used today in the Stockholm region. Of these 400 liters per capita per day, 200 are used for domestic purposes, about 100 by urban industry, and 100 for public sanitation, hospitals, and other amenities. In country areas about 200 liters per capita per day is a realistic figure. This includes livestock requirements. In the following calculations of total water requirements, moreover, the assumption is made for the sake of simplicity that half the inhabitants of each continent live in towns and cities and half in the countryside, which seems by all accounts to be a reasonable forecast for the year 2000.

The estimate just made for towns and cities is a conservative one, when compared with the amounts of water being used today in a large modern city in the United States. Taking New York as an example, we find that the daily per capita requirement rose from 430 liters per capita per day in 1900 to 500 liters just before the outbreak of the last war. By the end of the 1940s, the figure had risen to 700 liters per capita per day, but after a serious drought in 1949 vigorous water conservancy measures reduced it to about 450. By the mid-1960s, the daily per capita requirement had risen to 600, but after the severe drought of 1965, it was reduced again to about 500 liters. This figure is probably typical of a present-day city. In cities with a great deal of industry and where air conditioning is needed, total urban consumption can be 2,000 liters per capita per day.

How much water is needed for industrial purposes?

Water has a far greater dissolving power than any other substance, and therefore plays an important part in chemical industries, all the more so as it is cheap. In countries with small irrigation requirements, industry usually accounts for the greater part of water demand. Industrial water is used for a variety of purposes—as a solvent, for washing and rinsing, for cooling, and for the removal of dissolved or suspended substances. Typical figures for the amount of water used in the production of one ton of different commodities are as follows. Of course, the amount used depends on the production process employed, but as can be seen, the amount is often several hundred times the weight of the product being produced.

Nitrogenous			
fertilizer	600 m³/ton	Sugar	100 m³/ton
Steel	150 „	Artificial silk	1 000 „
Paper	250 „	Brick	2 „
Oil	180 „	Plastic	750—2 000 „

As a result of the widespread use of water in production processes and the rapid expansion of industry, industrial water consumption in the industrialized countries has risen very steeply during this century. By the mid-1960s it was about 1,800 liters per capita per day in Sweden, and about 3,000 per capita per day in the USA, while the world average, i.e., the entire industrial requirement divided by the world's population, was about 1,200 liters per capita per day.

This rapid rise, however, has led to a disastrous increase in the volume of industrial effluent. In many of the western countries, this has prompted severe water management regulations. At the same time, the stipulations calling for purification of industrial effluent have encouraged industry to reuse the water by putting it back into the production process after it has passed through a purification plant. As a result of this type of reuse, industrial water requirements, spread out over the entire national population, have been reduced in relation to output. However, as industrial output has risen in the meantime in Sweden, the total effect has been a standstill in industrial water demand per capita.

In estimating future industrial water requirements, consideration is given to two alternatives aimed at showing the need to restrain industrial water demand by means of recycling and other methods. In alternative *A* we assume that per capita water demand in industry corresponds to the amount of water used in Sweden today—which is a fairly extravagant alternative (1,400 liters per capita per day or 500 m³ per capita per annum). If this industrial water demand were to be applied more generally in the developing countries, it would soon result in *disastrous volumes of effluent.*

Within a mere 25 years, the total amount of waste water from communities and industry would be about 4,000 km³ per annum, i.e., more than 10 percent of total river runoff.

Thus, not even 1-in-10 dilution would then be possible on average. A situation of this kind would be disastrous, and in many continents all fresh water would, in practice, be polluted even if general purification standards were far higher than in the industries of the industrialized countries today.

Huge flows of sewage will force a change of policy

To avoid the gradual development of a pollution disaster during the next few decades, there is no choice but to implement a completely different water policy, above all in industry. The water requirements of developed industry must be reduced very severely by the gradual adoption of dry manufacturing processes. Indispensable water must be recycled, and purification requirements must be made more stringent. Economic thought must be adjusted to a more long-term perspective than it has today.

In alternative B it is assumed that, although future industry will require the same amount of water as in alternative A, 90 percent of this water will be recycled. The water intake, therefore, will be limited to what is needed to make up for water losses by evaporation, incorporation in the product, etc., during the manufacturing process (roughly 20 percent is assumed), and the 10 percent of effluent which could not be regenerated. In alternative B we obtain a water requirement which is $1 - 0.9 (1 - 0.2) = 0.28$, the water demand of alternative A, or 140 m³ per capita per annum.

Domestic and industrial water needs in twenty-five years' time

We can now work out the total amounts of water that will be required in the future to cater to the needs of the population and industry. The following table shows the requirements of different continents in twenty-five and forty years' time respectively. The figures are based on the population fore-

casts compiled within the UN prior to the Bucharest conference. Here, as elsewhere in this book, the USSR is treated
separately from Asia and Europe.

*Total water extraction requirements for population and
industry*

Continent	Population, millions			Total water needs, km³ per annum			
	1970	2000	2015	2000		2015	
				A	B	A	B
Africa	344	818	1 154	500	205	700	290
Asia, except USSR	2 056	3 778	4 684	2 310	945	2 850	1 170
Australia	19	35	43	21	9	26	11
Europe, except USSR	462	568	618	350	142	380	155
North America	228	333	380	205	83	230	95
South America	283	652	908	400	163	550	230
USSR	243	330	368	200	82	225	92

Comparing these figures with water supply as shown in the
table on page 17, we find that most continents have ample
margins, so long as we disregard irrigation requirements.
Even at this point, however, it is clear that water resources
will be under severe strain if alternative *A* is applied in Asia,
owing to the very large population of that continent. Asia's
industrialization will, therefore, have to be based on recircu-
lation from an early stage to make up for the scarcity of
water.

How much water will be needed for irrigation?

There are large areas of the world where, in average years at
least, rainfall is sufficient to meet agricultural requirements.

26

Many densely populated countries, however, are situated in the drier climatic zones. Many of them are poor countries, and their industrial output is far too small for them to be able to pay for imports of necessary foodstuffs from other climatic zones. If the dry countries are to be able to develop their food production sufficiently to feed their own populations, irrigation will be absolutely essential. Irrigation implies the artificial supply of water for vegetation to make up for the deficiencies of rainfall (cf. map on page 3).

About half the world's food production today is based on rain-fed agriculture. The other half is based on irrigation. Although the irrigated area is no more than about 15 percent of the total cultivated area, irrigation uses more water than the other two needs we have just been discussing, namely public water supply and industry. Lvovich estimates the present extraction for public water supply and industry at 310 km^3 per annum and the extraction for irrigation at 2,500 km^3 per annum.

Irrigation is bound to play a vital part in keeping the future population of the world reasonably well fed, because *water is a key factor in raising agricultural output*. This was already apparent to the world's early civilizations, when irrigation was an important field of public enterprise. As mentioned earlier, it has become clear in recent years that one of the reasons for the failure of the Green Revolution was that crops were still far too vulnerable to the caprices of natural water supply. Bad harvests can, to a very great extent, be attributed to a shortage or an excess of water. (Further to this point, see page 34.)

In India today 97 percent of all technically handled water is already being devoted to irrigation, and yet we can still read in the press about harvests failing because the monsoon is delayed. The situation in India is so precarious that a serious delay in the monsoon, or a water shortage due to extensive impairment of the quality of water, would immediately result in disastrous and widespread famine. It should be noted that moderate delays in rainfall can also have long-term effects, for if soil too long remains dry it may lose its fertility.

To arrive at a figure for the amount of water that will be needed in the future for irrigation purposes, we will start with the assumption that the irrigated area requires an average of 900 mm per harvest per annum. This makes 9,000 m³ per harvested hectare. The amount of this water which actually benefits the crops will depend on the magnitude of the losses occurring during the flow of water from the watercourse, or aquifer, to the plant. It is not uncommon today for this level of efficiency to be quite low—between 30 and 40 percent, because a great deal of water evaporates or percolates into the ground on its way from the extraction point to the field, and also because a great deal of water is lost in the field before it can benefit the plants (due to evaporation from the ground and water surfaces, percolation through the soil to the groundwater, and diversion by ditches). We have to assume, however, that future irrigation will be far more efficient than that practised today, and we will therefore assume that the total efficiency of irrigation can be raised to 80 percent. In this case 700 mm of the 900 will benefit the plant. A certain amount of surplus water is desirable in order to avoid the risk of soil salinization, which is a problem today, because no arrangements have been made for the removal from the soil of the salts which are left behind when the water evaporates.

The preliminary documents for the Bucharest conference included an estimate of the population which the earth would be capable of supporting in the best of circumstances. This estimate was based on a continent-by-continent inventory of total cultivable acreage for purely rain-fed farming and for rain-fed and irrigation farming combined. The inventory distinguishes between potentially cultivable acreage and potentially harvestable acreage. The difference is that the latter makes allowance for the fact that a certain proportion of cultivable acreage is capable of bearing more than one harvest a year. The Bucharest figures were based on a detailed investigation carried out in the United States prior to the "Water for Peace" conference held in Washington in 1967. This investigation involved an estimate of potentially cultivable acreages in different parts of the world and the length of the cultivation season if any water shortage could be remedied. Soil conditions, temperature, and humidity were taken into consideration. The Bucharest report distinguishes between two cases. Case I refers to the whole of the potentially harvestable acreage; case II to the portion of that acreage situated outside the humid tropics, the latter being the zone of very heavy rainfall where there is a surplus of water and farming is confronted by serious problems, due, among other things, to excessive leaching of the soil. We shall return to this point in a subsequent chapter. The problems of efficient farming in this zone have not yet been solved, and the zone has therefore been excluded from calculations.

The following table shows the potential acreage requiring irrigation in different parts of the world, both for the world as a whole (case I) and outside the humid tropics with due allowance for the fact that water is available in the area (case II). As can be seen, the total acreage which will require irrigation corresponds to 2,730 million hectares (Mha), of which 1,112 million are situated outside the humid tropics and have water available for irrigation purposes. Assuming 900 mm water per harvest, the water requirement for irrigation can reach 24,600 km³ per annum (case I) or 10,000 km³ per annum (case II).

Potential world population as estimated for the Bucharest conference

The table also includes figures concerning the potential populations which the various continents would be capable of supporting in the best of circumstances. The estimate of potential population refers to case II. It is assumed that each hectare can feed twelve persons, but it should be made clear that this is an extremely high figure based upon the assumption of a possible output of six tons of edible food per hectare, which is a very high standard of agricultural proficiency—attained today by highly mechanized farming in the United States. It is assumed, moreover, that each

Water requirements for the irrigation of the world's potential harvestable acreage (based on the Bucharest Report)

Continent	Potential irrigated harvested area (million hectares)		Potential population*	Water requirements (km³ per annum) for full irrigation	
	total	outside the humid tropics and with water available	1,000 millions		
	(Case I)	(Case II)		Case I	Case II
Africa	1 160	290	9,48		2 610
Asia, except USSR	630	510	13,20		4 590
Australia	180	2	1,82		18
Europe, except USSR	40	40	3,24		360
North America	210	160	9,00		1 440
South America	480	80	7,20		720
USSR	30	30	4,80		270
Whole world	2 730	1 112	48,7	24 600	10 000

*Calculated without allowance for the availability of water.

individual requires the equivalent of 4,000 or 5,000 kcal per day; the diet also has to include protein, fruit, etc., which somewhat raises the true calory intake requirement. These calculations led to the conclusion that the earth was capable of feeding a potential population totaling 48 billion, which is more than ten times the present figure.

There are, of course, several possible objections to this argument. The most interesting objection for our purposes is that no investigation was made to find out if there would be enough water. We shall return to this shortly.

The above table showed that the water required for the potential acreage which could be harvested—i.e., 2,730 mega-hectares (Mha) altogether, including 1,112 Mha outside the humid tropics—was roughly 24,600 and 10,000 km³ per annum (cases I and II respectively). To this is added the water required for domestic and industrial purposes. It will be recalled that the former required an average of 300 liters per capita per day, corresponding to 110 m³ per capita per annum, while the latter required either 500 m³ per annum (alternative *A*) or 140 m³ per annum (alternative *B*). For a maximum world population of 48 billion, the total domestic and industrial water requirements for alternative *A* will be 29,300 km³ per annum, and for case *B* (90 percent recycling) they will be 12,000 km³ per annum. Adding these figures to the irrigation requirement, we find that the total amount of water needed for domestic, industrial, and irrigation needs, according to the two cultivation alternatives I and II, is as follows:

Alternative	Water requirement, km³ per annum	% of total runoff
I A	53 900	139
I B	36 600	94
II A	39 300	102
II B	22 000	57

As can be seen from the final column, water resources would be exceeded in alternative *A,* while in case *B* (90 percent recycling) between about 55 and 95 percent of global water resources would be needed. These are, of course, frighteningly high percentages. The figures show that the population to be fed cannot be computed solely on the basis of a discussion of potentially cultivable soil, as was done prior to the Bucharest conference. The general observation that water is needed for agricultural production is not enough. Consideration must also be given to the amounts of water which are required in order to cover the simultaneous water requirements of society and industry. It then becomes evident that the quantities needed are unrealistically large. It is important to emphasize that the exploitation of large quantities of water is bound to involve serious technical problems. Moreover, the environmental repercussions would create very serious conflict situations.

Water needs for different sizes of world population

One is naturally moved to ask how trustworthy findings of this kind can be. One way of answering the question is to make comparisons with previous estimates. One such estimate was made at the Athens School of Ekistics by Nikitopoulos and published in 1962. Nikitopoulos was also interested in calculating the potential size of the world's population and its distribution between different continents. He presumed a domestic need of 192 m³ per capita per annum, and an industrial requirement of the same magnitude. He assumed the irrigation requirement to average 700 m³ per capita per annum. This makes a total average requirement of 1,084 m³ per capita per annum.

Concerning global water supply, Nikitopoulos estimated that it would be possible to utilize 18,000 km³ per annum of the total quantity available, which he estimated at 26,200 km³ per annum, i.e., corresponding to a utilization of approximately 70 percent. In this way, Nikitopoulos arrived at the conclusion that our planet could support 19 billion people, if water supply was assumed to determine the limit of population growth. We also took into consideration the additional supply of water obtainable through the desalinization of seawater. Since the major water needs are in the remote interiors of the continents, to which it would be too expensive to convey desalinized water, it would not be economically feasible to desalinize more than 2,140 km³ seawater per annum. Thus, given an adequate supply of energy, not more than about 10 percent of water needs could be satisfied by means of desalinization.

Estimates by various writers (see figure above) suggest that a reasonable total per capita water requirement for the future may be between 900 and 1,300 m³ per annum. Let us now once again assume that we can use 70 percent of the available amount of water, i.e., 27,000 km³ per annum. In this case, the

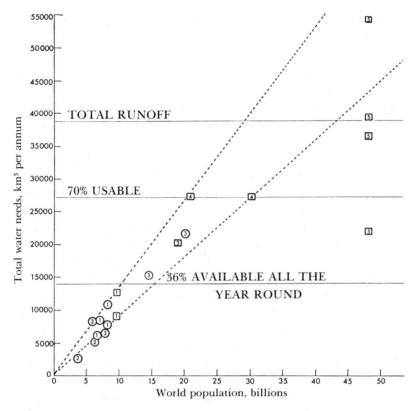

Various estimates of the total water needs of the world's population.
The squares denote estimates of potential world population.
The figures denote (4) authors: (1) Falkenmark-Lindh, (2) Lvovich, (3) Nikitopoulos, (5) preparatory documents for the Bucharest conference.

available supply would clearly be sufficient for about 25 billion people. The fact is that this corresponds to a mere 50 percent of the potential world population which emerged as a result of the above-mentioned calculations prior to the UN World Population Conference in Bucharest (see fig.). The differences between the potential world population figures quoted here are mainly due to different assumptions having been made concerning water requirements for different purposes and concerning the size of the available water supply.

Water needs and water resources in different parts of the world

Having obtained some idea of the relationship between water needs and population at a global level, we return to the distribution of water between different parts of the world. A study of this kind will, of course, provide a more accurate picture of the relationship between water and population, since it will bring out regional variations which reflect the uneven spatial distribution of water. In the table on page 17, we saw how water resources varied from one continent to another. The figures on pages 35 and 36 show the relationship between water needs—as percentages of total runoff—and population in Africa, Asia, Europe, North America, South America, and the USSR. The curves in the figures refer to case II *A*, which we discussed earlier. The figure also includes the stable part of runoff, which is also expressed as a percentage of total runoff. It will be recalled that stable runoff is an important concept in this context, because it corresponds to the quantity which we can always expect to have at our disposal. We shall also assume that there is no recycling of water in the industrial sector.

The curves show that by about the year 2100, water needs in Africa will have caught up with the quantity available for use from stable runoff. In Asia we can see that water needs will have caught up with stable runoff by about 1990. In other parts of the world it will be a long time before water demand equals stable runoff.

We may conclude that, if stable runoff is taken as a yardstick of water supply, the situation in Asia will soon be extremely precarious. This will apply to Africa in just over a hundred years' time.

The pressure on our water resources will very soon be a problem

It is, of course, only natural to ask what difficulties are likely to arise as the extreme water needs mentioned above are

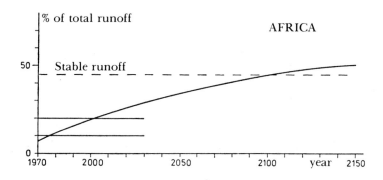

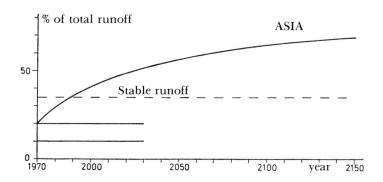

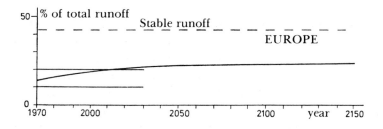

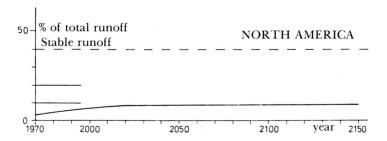

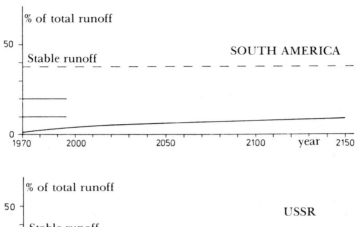

Water needs—as percentages of total runoff—in different continents, given the present-day living standards indicated in the text (Asia and Europe excluding the USSR). Horizontal lines indicate Balcerski's 10 percent and 20 percent limits. See also page 40.

approached. Efforts have been made to answer this question, one of the leading workers in this field being a Polish scientist, Balcerski. By studying water situations in European countries (discussed later), Balcerski has worked out the way in which the degree of water utilization influences an economy. Briefly, his findings are as follows.

The prospects of solving questions of water supply may be termed favorable as long as water needs are less than 5 percent of total runoff. It is only in densely populated areas that difficulties can conceivably arise, and even these are judged to be of a transitory nature.

The prospects of solving questions of water supply are generally still favorable even if water demand amounts to between 5 and 10 percent of total runoff, but there is an increase in the number of areas destined to encounter temporary difficulties, and plans have to be drawn up for regional water supplies in certain vulnerable areas or groups of areas.

If water demand rises to between 10 and 20 percent, water supply can be said to constitute a problem. General planning has to be resorted to, and heavy investments have to be made for the solution of water supply problems.

Finally, if water demand exceeds 20 percent of total runoff, in the area under consideration, questions of water supply can be described as the absolute limiting factor of economic development. In other words, water management plays such an important part in the economy of the country or area that it completely dominates economic planning.

Armed with this information concerning the influence gradually exerted on the economic situation and, consequently, on the prosperity of the country or area, we shall now proceed to a new analysis of the relationships shown by the curves in the previous figure. To the figures on pages 35 and 36 we have now added straight lines marking 10 and 20 percent limits to the utilization of total runoff. What effect do these limits have on our assessment of the water situation?

As far as Asia is concerned on this basis the situation is very much worse. It looks as though the point of 20 percent utilization of total runoff has been passed. This possibly surprising assertion implies that the pressure on water supplies in Asia will produce a precarious situation without any population increase, given the improved standards of domestic, industrial, and agricultural water use outlined previously. Our conclusion must be that questions of water supply are crucial to the economic development of this part of the world. In fact, the last few years have confirmed the problems of food supply which India and Pakistan, for example, have had to contend with, due not least to the fluctuations of water supply caused by the monsoons. We shall return to these problems in chapter 5.

Africa appears to be passing the 10 percent level now, and the 20 percent level will have been reached by the year 2000, given the water needs we have outlined. We can therefore expect deepening problems of water supply in Africa during the next few decades.

Europe too would seem to have already passed the 10

percent level, and the 20 percent limit seems likely to be reached in about the year 2010. Here as well, therefore, we can expect a difficult water supply situation to arise after the next few decades.

Mean values are only mean values

It is important to emphasize once more that our argument is based on mean values for the various continents. Within the various continents there is, of course, a wide distribution around the mean values of water needs in relation to water supply, which we have been discussing. The uneven spatial distribution of water is illustrated by Sweden in relation to Europe. At present, our water supply situation is such that water needs in relation to the country's total water supply could be characterized by a percentage which is far less than ten and is therefore below the continental mean. The statistical distribution is made still clearer by a study of the remaining three curves in the figure. North America, South America, and the USSR appear unlikely to encounter any problems of water supply within the foreseeable future, but we know that some parts of North America have already experienced disturbing crises of water supply. This suggests that a presentation based on mean values conveys a picture which, to a greater or lesser extent, underestimates the difficulties involved. Then again, our figures concerning individual water needs were very conservative. For instance, they provide no scope for the water requirements of air conditioning. We shall consider these points in a subsequent chapter in which we appraise the water supply problems of the industrialized countries.

What will be the result of increasing industrial reuse of water?

So far, in considering the water situation of different parts of the world, our attitude concerning Asia, Africa, and Europe has been one of empirical pessimism. How is this situation to be brought under control? We start by considering the possibilities of changing water policy, and the effects which a different approach would have upon the conclusions which have already been drawn. Apart from, say, restricting household demand for water, the most radical measure would be for industry to try to reuse water after having purified it to an extent compatible with industrial technology. Previously we discussed an alternative which we termed alternative *B*, and which presupposed 90 percent reuse of industrial water. To illustrate the conceivable effects on water supply conditions of different degrees of reuse, we have shown in the figure on page 40 the effect of reuse between 0 and 90 percent on the results presented earlier. This experiment has been confined to Europe and Asia.

In the case of Europe we find that greater reuse may improve the water supply situation. But we find also that, in time, this regeneration of water will have to amount to almost 90 percent in order to meet an acceptable level of water demand.

The water supply situation in Asia will improve somewhat, but we will already have passed the 20 percent level by the turn of the century, even if the degree of reuse is as high as 90 percent. Clearly, then, a change of water policy cannot be confined to the industrial reuse of water. Industry will have to develop methods that are more economical of water, and irrigation must be made more efficient.

Flood water can be stored in huge reservoirs

From what we have already said, it is clear that in South and East Asia, for instance, parts of the unstable water supply will have to be captured. In other words, efforts must be made to utilize the quantities of water that are available in the rivers for only short periods because of floods, i.e., water over and above the quantity we have termed the stable part. One such enterprise would be to capture the great floods which inundate parts of Bangladesh after heavy rains. This

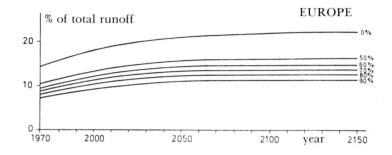

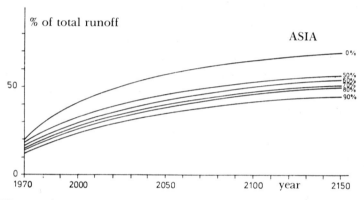

Water needs—as percentages of total runoff—at different degrees of regeneration in Europe and Asia (except the USSR).

would, among other things, necessitate the construction of great dams capable of enclosing the required quantities. Dams or reservoirs of this kind need not always be constructed aboveground. Underground constructions are quite feasible, and, in fact, are preferable in areas of heavy evaporation. To arrive at the number of dams which might have to be built, it is worth knowing that Lake Nasser—the lake formed by the Aswan Dam—has an active reservoir of about 130 km³ between the highest and lowest water levels. By way of comparison, the nonstable part of the water resources of South and East Asia, according to one of the previous tables, is about 6,650 km³, i.e., fifty times as large. Fifty reservoirs the size of Lake Nasser would therefore be needed to make

40

this amount of water available for water supply.

As we all know, however, the construction of big reservoirs gives rise to a series of environmental problems. It is already clear that Lake Nasser has extensively disrupted the ecological balance of the Nile. The lessons of these events must be acted on if we are not to exchange our problems of water supply for a number of equally, if not more, difficult problems of an environmental nature. Let us pause to consider some of the effects which have followed in the wake of the Aswan Dam and Lake Nasser. The High Dam, which is built across the Nile, has a volume several times that of the Great Pyramid. Before the dam was built, the Nile would overflow its banks every year between July and October as a result of the summer rains in Ethiopia. This had the effect of distributing soil from the fertile basalt lava of Ethiopia, over the Nile valley and delta. This supply of soil was one of the principal foundations of the civilizations which flourished along the Nile. (Further to this point, see chapter 3.)

Many problems to be solved

The soil carried by the water into the Nile delta also encouraged the growth of algae and fish off the Mediterranean coast as far away as Lebanon to the northeast. It has been possible to study the effect of high water floods on the production process in the Nile delta. For example, certain algae cells, which might amount to 35,000 cells per liter in the delta estuary before the Nile flood, had risen to 2,400,000 cells per liter afterwards. These algae cells provided food for sardines, among other creatures. Before the Aswan Dam was built, sardine catches were estimated at 18,000 tons a year.

Now that the High Dam has been built, the soil is trapped as sediment in the reservoir. Consequently, the farmers downstream are now having to use large quantities of fertilizer. The United Arab Republic is in the fortunate position of having good supplies of phosphate, and electricity generated at the Aswan Dam can be used for the manufacture of nitrate. It has been estimated, however, that it will cost over $114 million per annum to replace the fertile soil from Ethiopia. The problem of diminishing sardine catches is less easily solved. Catches have now fallen to 500 tons a year, though, of course, fishing in Lake Nasser provides a certain measure of compensation.

Downstream of the dam, the Nile no longer carries any soil with the result that the delta is gradually shrinking, because the soil carried out to sea is no longer being replaced. There is also a serious risk of the brackish-water lakes, now forming buffer zones on the fringe of the delta zone near the Mediterranean, gradually becoming salinized. If they do, large areas of fertile land will be lost.

But perhaps the most serious ecological repercussion is that Lake Nasser has become a source of water-borne diseases. It is, above all, the various parasites carried by snails which have now acquired greater opportunities for reproduction through the construction of Lake Nasser. These parasites cause skin diseases, debility, eye diseases, and other complaints.

Other problems generated by large storage reservoirs aboveground include heavy evaporation. It has been estimated that about 10 percent of the water in Lake Nasser is lost every year. Another problem is connected with the installation having to serve a multitude of purposes. At the same time as the reservoir is used for the generation of electricity, it has to provide the area downstream with water for irrigation. Industrial water demand is practically constant all the year round, while agricultural requirements vary a great deal from one season to another. Water demand is much higher in summer than in winter, for instance. If these fluctuations of agricultural demand are taken into account, optimum utilization for industry becomes impossible. If, on the other hand, industrial requirements are given priority, farmers get too much water in winter and not enough in summer.

Water regulation projects require many different experts

In this chapter we have discussed the possibility of utilizing the whole of the stable part of water supply—as we will have to do in certain parts of the world in order to cater to water needs. The necessary technical measures can be expected to have serious repercussions on the external environment, and it is very important for such projects to be planned with full awareness of the risks of ecological consequences. It is particularly important for a close study to be made of the effect of short-term solutions, because solutions of this kind have often been resorted to in order to solve short-term problems of supply. No negative consequences have been feared within the framework of the short-term plan, but there have been a number of cases where, naturally enough, the ecological consequences have produced unexpected repercussions over a somewhat longer period of time. This has led to the conclusion—a conclusion which should be taken into account in all research—that planning should be conducted to the greatest possible extent on a long-term basis. Long-term planning also means, of course, that efforts must be made to predict the ecological consequences of a project. Without a long-term plan of this kind, one is liable, following the execution of short-term measures, to be faced with the task of solving secondary environmental problems which could have been avoided if the project had been organized on a long-term basis from the very outset. The solutions of secondary environmental problems of this kind can be of such proportions and of such a nature as to force the abandonment of a logically constructed long-term plan whose implementation has perhaps already begun.

3   *Water and agriculture*

As we have already observed, the banal truth is that all organic life is dependent on access to water. Man himself needs water for drinking, cooking, hygienic purposes, industrial production, and so on. Animals, too, cannot possibly survive without access to water. But it is plants that consume by far the greatest quantities.

Owing to the water requirements of plant life, the agricultural potential of areas with little rainfall is always limited by water supply. As long ago as 3000 B.C., people began building channels to water the fields in dry areas. This called for technical knowledge, on the basis of which great civilizations arose. The civilizations of Mesopotamia, the Nile, the Indus and Ganges, and the river valleys of China are all well-known examples of this process. From an early age, therefore, man lived in a state of technical equilibrium with the water of the rivers and the cultivated and irrigated fields.

Plants must have water

Why does a plant need water? First and foremost, water is one of the raw materials used to build up plant substance. This is because water plays a part in the fundamental chemical process of the plant kingdom, that known as photosynthesis or carbon dioxide assimilation. In this process, which is essential to all living things, carbon dioxide and water are converted with the aid of light energy into carbohydrates, the gross formula for this reaction being:

carbon dioxide+water+light energy=sugar+oxygen

Apart from serving as a raw material, water is also needed in plants to act as a solvent and as a physical building element. Together with the substances dissolved, water stretches the soft tissues in a plant to keep the plant upright. Turgidity also plays a part in other processes, for instance, when the plant presses the points of its roots through the soil.

A plant does not need very large quantities of water for these purposes. The large quantities of water are needed for another process. In this process, a constant stream of water flows up from the roots to the leaves, where it is discharged into the atmosphere as water vapor through millions of small openings called stomata. It is also through these openings that the plant absorbs the necessary carbon dioxide from the atmosphere. When sunlight shines on the leaves, the stomata open to facilitate carbon dioxide assimilation, but at the same time the plant loses large quantities of water as a result of the evaporation which is made possible by the opening of the stomata.

The passage of water through the plant in connection with evaporation is not so much a part of the "inner life" of the plant as a consequence of the plant having to open the surfaces of its leaves in order to absorb atmospheric carbon dioxide. Evaporation or transpiration is proportional to assimilation, which in turn regulates growth, and evaporation for Swedish farm crops is estimated at 400-800 kg water per kg of growth. Evaporation is generally far heavier from a planted field than from a bare one. If we assume, for instance, that the production of dry matter from a field of wheat is 7,000 g per hectare, this will involve a water consumption of about 4 million kg, corresponding to 400 mm precipitation. In round figures, this equals the annual precipitation in those parts of Sweden with the lowest rainfall.

The amount of water a plant needs per kg of growth varies according to circumstances. Thus, water consumption is increased by high temperatures and heavy evaporation, and it is also thought to increase if a plant suffers from a deficiency of some other nutrient. In the latter case, the plant will pump up more water from the ground to absorb as much as possible of the substance it is short of. A plant also has a certain capacity to adjust its water consumption to the supply, at the same time that it has a tendency to waste water when the supply is plentiful.

Different plant species have very different requirements for water supply. Xerophytes, which grow in dry zones, are equipped with various transpiration-prevention devices. For example, their leaves may be covered by a waxy layer, or their stomata may be protected from the wind by hairs. These plants often have very deep roots reaching down to the groundwater. Hydrophytes, the antithesis of xerophytes, are plants which need a lot of water and which grow in places where there is a lot of moisture. Cultivated plants occupy an intermediate position between xerophytes and hydrophytes. One exception to this rule is rice, which grows in places where there is a surplus of water.

The plant adapts itself to the supply of water

Depending on water supply, plants fall into different types of plant communities, which are adapted to the water supply of the particular habitat. In Sweden it is possible to distinguish four main types or series of hydrologically determined plant communities, namely the moorland series, the steppe series, the meadow series, and the wetland series. Each of these series includes both treeless communities and woodland. Outside Sweden there are, of course, many other series, e.g., in dry zones the desert series, incorporating species which flourish in extremely dry conditions.

The water supply on which vegetation has to draw is not constant. On the contrary, it can vary a great deal from time to time. Dry periods alternate with rainy ones, and usually this alternation is fairly regular throughout the year. For instance, large areas of the semiarid zones alternate regularly between three- to six-month periods of complete drought and periods of good precipitation. The plants, animals, and people living in these areas are completely adapted to this rhythm. Sometimes, however, this regular cycle is disrupted, either by droughts lasting for a whole year (if not several years), or else by surplus precipitation which devastates the vegetation.

What makes it possible for plant life to adjust to these variable conditions? Above all, it is the ability of the soil to store water on which plants can survive during periods of drought. For the most part, this water is not groundwater. It is water trapped in the soil in the form of soil moisture, i.e., the water which adheres to the individual particles of soil, forming a layer of moisture around them, and which also forms small menisci between the individual grains. This is the water which the ground rapidly absorbs when it rains and which makes the ground moist. Plants are capable of detaching this soil moisture down to a limit which we call the *wilting point*. When all the water above this limit has been absorbed by the plants, the water which remains adheres so firmly to the soil particles that it cannot be detached by the roots, and the plants die.

Different types of soil can retain very different amounts of water. Roughly speaking, fine soils such as clays can retain large amounts of water. Thus a meter-thick stratum of clay can hold anything up to one year's Swedish precipitation, which will keep plants supplied with water for long periods of drought. Sandy soil does not have anything like this capacity, and it is a well-known fact that sandy soils are usually sensitive to drought.

Plants also need oxygen

We have now discussed the importance of water to vegetation, and the inference might seem to be that, the better the supply of water, the better the prospects for plant life. This is true, but only up to a certain point. Other factors intervene and set a limit to vegetation growth. Oxygen supply is one such factor. Ordinary land plants need access to oxygen in the soil for root respiration. If there is no oxygen available, a plant will suffocate. Water and air—or rather, water and oxygen—compete with one another for space in the cavities of the soil. If there is too much water in the soil, this will limit the oxygen supply, and plant life will suffer damage as a result.

Hydrophites, such as reeds and horse-tails, are an exception to this rule. They have a built-in ventilation system in their roots which makes them independent of soil oxygen. Rice is another such plant. Taking land plants as a whole, the dependence of growth on the supply of water and oxygen in the soil can be illustrated by a diagram of the kind shown in the following figure. As will be seen, there is an optimum point for growth, namely the point of intersection between the two growth curves. This optimum may be differently situated in the case of different plants, but the majority of cultivated plants flourish best when about half the pores of the soil are filled with air.

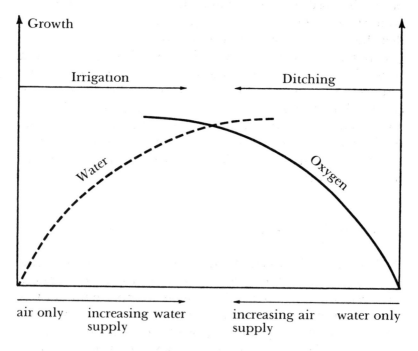

The dependence of growth on air and water. If there is a shortage of water, irrigation is resorted to. If instead there is a shortage of air, drainage is resorted to in order to remove superfluous water and enable air to reach the root zone.

Our argument so far has shown that two distinct measures may be necessary in order to bring about a significant increase of crops from the cultivated land in the world. If there is a shortage of water, this means that we are to the left of the optimum point in the above figure and that irrigation is needed to improve growth. If, on the other hand, we have a surplus of water in the ground, drainage is required—not because the water is poisonous to the plants in any way, but because it excludes oxygen from the soil, thereby stifling the plants. Drainage, then, has to be undertaken in order to make more room in the soil for atmospheric oxygen.

Irrigation and drainage—both are needed

Irrigation and drainage are thus complementary operations. The predominance of one or the other in a particular situation will above all else depend on climate, but also on the type of soil and other factors. In Sweden, for instance, where precipitation is generally satisfactory and fairly evenly distributed throughout the year, and where evaporation is limited due to the low prevailing temperature, there is generally a surplus of water as far as cultivated plants are concerned. Drainage is therefore the overwhelmingly predominant means of regulation in Swedish agriculture. Ever since it was first introduced into Sweden by the Cistercians during the 12th and 13th centuries, drainage has occupied a prominent position in Swedish agricultural technology and has even been made the subject of special legislation. Especially during the 19th century, when in spite of heavy emigration the population of the country doubled and the cultivated acreage quadrupled, drainage was of fundamental importance to Swedish food supply. Similar developments can be traced in other countries with climates similar to that of Sweden. Even today, ditching still plays an important part in Sweden, although it is little publicized. It has been estimated that Sweden has about 600,000 km of open drainage ditches, which means that end-to-end they could extend 15 times round the equator. The efficiency and maintenance of these ditches are two of the essential preconditions of agriculture in Sweden.

Although farmers in Sweden have used ditches in their fields and still do so, irrigation is also needed in some parts of the country. Precipitation is particularly meager at times in the southeast. This region is normally afflicted by what the farmers call an early summer drought. Irrigation can be worthwhile in a situation of this kind, although ditching is also necessary. Interest in irrigation has risen markedly in recent years. Increasing interest and competition are being focused on the summer water of the lakes and rivers of the plains. The main reason for this rising interest in irrigation is that large sums of money are invested by farmers nowadays in every crop in the form of the cost-of-land capital, seed, fertilizer, and labor. With so much at stake, a failed harvest can be a financial disaster. Thus, irrigation is important even in a well-watered country like Sweden.

However, it is in other countries, in the arid and semiarid zones of the world, that irrigation and water supply become crucial to plant production. It is only when one visits these areas that the importance of water as a factor in human food production becomes fully apparent. There are large areas where plant production and farming simply would not exist if it were not for irrigation. If irrigation were not possible, the population of these countries would be reduced to the merest fraction of its present size. Even in countries whose climate is only partially arid or semiarid, development opportunities are still closely bound up with availability of water supply. For example, as we have already had occasion to observe, no less than 97 percent of all the water technically handled in India is applied to irrigation and, therefore, to food production.

Water and salt

Cultivated plants require not only a certain amount of water but also water of a certain quality. Above all, the salt content of the water must not exceed a certain limit. If it does, the plants will be unable to absorb the water. Different plants pose different requirements in this respect. Sugar beets, for instance, which are descended from a beach plant, will tolerate up to 0.5 percent salt content, which means that they can be given water from the Baltic. Other plants, e.g., citrus species, react negatively to a far lower salt content. Seawater, therefore, can never be used directly for irrigation. Saltwater irrigation can damage soil as well as plants. When saltwater is supplied to the soil and the water evaporates, either directly or through the plants, the salt accumulates in the soil and ultimately ruins it.

This is one of the really serious problems arising out of irrigation in conditions of drought. All natural water contains at least a minute quantity of salt. When water is transferred to a desert area for irrigation purposes and evaporates, the salt is always left behind in the soil, because there is insufficient rainfall to wash the soil clean. Although the salt may only occur in minute quantities in the irrigation water, it gradually accumulates in the soil. At one time, for example, West Pakistan was losing 25,000 hectares of fertile land a year because of this type of salinization. In Peru today, nearly 10 percent of the cultivated acreage has been damaged by salinization. Other areas similarly affected include the Imperial Valley and the Colorado Basin in the United States, the Mexicali Valley in Northern Mexico, and the area between the Tigris and Euphrates in Syria and Iraq.

One way of avoiding salinization is to supply more irrigation water than the plants can absorb, so that a certain amount of rinsing water is left over. Various surveys have shown that approximately a 25 percent surplus is needed. This surplus, however, must be drained off after it has been used for washing the soil. Irrigation, therefore, has to be combined with drainage in order for the arrangement to work properly. Drainage of this kind is often difficult, due, among other things, to gradient problems. A typical example of such problems is provided by large areas of the Indus valley, where the drop from the foothills of the Himalayas to the coast is less than 300 meters over a distance of 800 km, giving a gradient of less than 0.05 percent. Natural drainage is hardly feasible in a situation of this kind.

Instead, the salt-laden surplus water from irrigation lingers in the irrigated area and percolates down into the ground-water, which in many instances already contains salt. As a result, large areas of land are simultaneously waterlogged and salinized.

The risk of waterlogging

Irrigation is complicated in another respect too. It has been found, for instance, in modern irrigation works in the Punjab area that water has leaked out of unlined irrigation channels, and raised the water table seven to ten meters above a level which had been relatively stable since 1835. This rise in the water table occurred during the first ten years the irrigation system was in use.

The frequent occurrence of salinization and waterlogging as a result of irrigation is a major global problem in the agricultural sector. It is now estimated that, on a world basis, between 200,000 and 300,000 hectares of irrigated land are lost every year due to salinization and waterlogging. At a rough guess, some 20-25 million hectares of land which have now been destroyed by salinization were once fertile farmland. Unfortunately, this destruction is partly due to human folly and incompetence. In theory at least, experts now know how these adverse effects can be avoided.

First and foremost, efforts are made to improve the situation by means of new irrigation and drainage techniques which, among other things, involve the use of pumping arrangements. It is important for drainage works to be installed at the same time as irrigation works, but they are often postponed for economic reasons.

There are large areas of the world where the problems of waterlogging are extremely difficult to solve. This is especially true of low-lying desert areas, where the cost of large-scale drainage works is generally prohibitive.

Other adverse consequences of irrigation

Another adverse effect of irrigation is the dissemination of waterborne diseases. Millions of people and animals are affected. In tropical and semitropical areas one finds that irrigation systems have actually fostered the development and the environment of parasites and waterborne pathogenic bacteria. Malaria, schistosomiasis, and liver diseases are spread in this way. These diseases were already known under the pharaohs, but at that time there existed something of an equilibrium. This equilibrium has been disturbed since irrigation became possible all the year round and was extended to increasingly large areas. Formerly, waterborne diseases were only virulent during rainy periods, receding somewhat during dry periods. Today there are parts of the world where these diseases are widespread. For example, studies conducted in Egypt have shown that in heavily infected areas the life expectancy of men and women is now only twenty-seven and twenty-five years respectively. It has also been shown that in the Sudan, following the introduction of all-the-year-round irrigation in a 350,000-hectare area in Gezira, there was a steep rise in diseases of the blood among both human beings and livestock.

The progressively more intensive use of fertilizers in agriculture has also created problems, because very small portions of nutrients are sufficient to cause algal bloom (15/1,000m. for phosphorus and 0.3 millionths for nitrogen). The great danger, of course, is that large quantities of surplus water from an irrigation installation can be discharged into a river or lake. Farmers often tend to spread overdoses of fertilizer in the belief that this will improve the yield. Damage of this kind to lakes and rivers is liable to be extensive. It is possible, however, that these problems will increase more slowly as fertilizers become more and more expensive. The best way of avoiding damage to lakes and rivers is to avoid the distribution of more than the optimum amount of fertilizer for the crop concerned. In this way environmental damage will be avoided, and the amount of nutrients supplied to watercourses will be kept to a minimum.

Where does irrigation water come from?

It is often overlooked that, compared with other technical purposes involving the use of water, irrigation demands enormous quantities. We saw in a previously quoted example that a wheat crop in Swedish climatic conditions can take up to 4,000 tons of water per hectare, the equivalent of 400 mm of precipitation. Two crops per year are common in arid and semiarid conditions; at the same time the hotter climate creates a heavier consumption of water per crop. Water demand for a single productive hectare can then amount to 15,000 m³, or 1,500 mm, per annum. A rice crop requires even more water, and intensive cultivation can involve twice the water consumption quoted above.

Where does the water that is needed for the irrigation of large areas come from? Primarily it is extracted from *rivers and lakes*—if there are any lakes. Unfortunately, however, the period of maximum water demand for irrigation, e.g., during six-month periods of drought between monsoons, often coincides with periods of low river flow, when water supplies are at their lowest. This has prompted several major water regulation projects in different parts of the world aimed at improving opportunities for irrigation. Most such projects have included large dam constructions, the aim being, more often than not, to provide a source of electrical power as well as irrigation. The Bhakra and Aswan dam projects on the Indus and Nile respectively are two projects of this kind. To make the water from these great catchment systems available for use in the fields, heavy follow-up investments usually have to be made in canals which often extend hundreds of kilometers through the area to be irrigated. Other necessary arrangements include sluices, terraces, and drainage systems.

In many places these follow-up investments have unfortunately failed to materialize, leaving the countries concerned with expensive but useless main systems. There are examples in India and elsewhere of major catchment enterprises and main irrigation systems which have stood idle for decades, because no finance has been forthcoming for the necessary ancillary investments. Again, the utilization of these systems has sometimes been partly or completely prevented by political or administrative considerations, e.g., riparian disputes between different countries or between member states of a single federation.

Too often have great irrigation systems been paralyzed for lack of maintenance or because of their negative consequences. The silting-up of regulating dams has proved to be a difficult problem. This has curtailed the service lives of even large dams. A similar problem, unheard of until only a year or two ago, has been generated by the water hyacinth, originally a Latin American plant, which has propagated to an alarming degree, particularly in man-made reservoirs. Finally, various profound problems of a social or cultural nature are liable to result from major irrigation enterprises. This has happened in the Nile Valley, where the Aswan Dam has completely transformed the flow of the river. This transformation has had severe repercussions on the lives of millions of people, whose customs and habits for thousands of years had been attuned to the regular alternations of river level between low water and flood.

Groundwater is another source of agricultural water supply. In fact, groundwater usually occurs in larger quantities than surface water. Altogether no less than 94 percent of the water reserves of the land surface consist of groundwater. On the other hand, the turnover and renewal rates of groundwater are much lower than those of surface water. The surface water in a river is replaced perhaps within a few days, while the corresponding process where groundwater is concerned may take thousands of years. Groundwater is usually of good enough quality for irrigation purposes, but sometimes it may be salt; this poses formidable complications.

Groundwater is greatly in demand for irrigation in many parts of the world, particularly in arid regions with few lakes and rivers. There is, for example, a single area in the south of India—roughly the size of Vermont—with more than

100,000 irrigation wells. Each well supplies no more than one or two hectares, but these mini-installations are immensely important, because groundwater used for irrigation has a number of significant advantages over surface water:

1. Groundwater may be available locally and can therefore be extracted without any serious transport problems.
2. Groundwater-extraction works, such as wells, can be developed successively as water demand increases. Consequently, there is no need for heavy preinvestments, as for dams.
3. Groundwater may occur in underground reservoirs which are big enough to provide supplies over several years of drought. The disastrous droughts that have occurred in recent years in Africa and Latin America would doubtless have been several times worse if there had not been groundwater reservoirs to fall back on.
4. Groundwater is shielded from evaporation and, therefore, does not disappear even if it is stored for hundreds of years. It is usually protected from surface pollution and is usually, therefore, of good quality.

On the other hand, the use of groundwater has disadvantages. One such disadvantage arises when more groundwater is extracted than infiltrates through the soil as a result of precipitation. This lowers the groundwater table and ultimately may empty the groundwater reservoir—a problem which is becoming more and more serious in dry zones. In recent years, large amounts of groundwater have been discovered at great depths in some desert areas, e.g., in Libya, and it is possible with modern drilling and pumping techniques for this water to be extracted. We shall return to this point in the chapter on Africa. The problem is that this groundwater is very old. It infiltrated between 20,000 and 50,000 years ago, during the Ice Age in northern Europe, at a time when there was abundant precipitation where there are now deserts. Today there is very little infiltration or none at all, and when the water is exhausted, the activities dependent on it—crop cultivation, stock breeding, or industry, as the case may be—will have to be discontinued. This may result in abandoned communities resembling the ghost towns adjoining worked-out mines in Latin America. It is important to know the magnitude of reserves, so that plans can be made for this development. Sometimes the situation can be serious, if it is found that the water will last for only a few years. In other areas the supply is expected to last for hundreds of years, so long as extraction is kept within limits.

What other water resources besides surfacewater and groundwater are available for irrigation? Faced with this question, one is tempted to think in terms of the *desalinization of seawater*, but a number of surveys in recent years have reached quite discouraging conclusions about this possibility. A summary, compiled in 1970 in the United States just before the onset of the fuel crisis, showed that the cost of desalinized seawater was at least ten times too great for it to be a feasible proposition for irrigation purposes. On the other hand, it was thought to be acceptable, where justified, as a source of public water supply. The rising energy costs generated by the fuel crisis have probably made desalinization even more uneconomical for irrigation purposes. The situation may change in the future. If we are heading for a major international expansion in the nuclear power sector, the use of surplus energy for the desalinization of seawater for irrigation may be an attractive proposition.

Rising world starvation calls for effective countermeasures

So far we have considered water and food production only in terms of the present-day situation. What kind of situation lies ahead? What are our chances of increasing food production to keep up with the rapid growth of world population? We touched on these questions in more general terms in the previous chapter, and we have already seen that questions concerning future population developments and future food production were recently discussed at two much-publicized UN conferences, namely the UN World Population Conference in Bucharest and the UN Food Conference in Rome. In connection with the latter, a great deal of expert material was compiled which in many ways offers more concrete information on the questions with which we are concerned here. A fairly penetrating survey was made of current and future food production in the world. The estimates referred to developing countries with market economies; developing countries with planned economies were excluded for the simple reason that no data were available.

In the material for the Rome conference, 1985 was taken as a "horizon year," an attempt being made to discuss the development of the population-food supply relationship up to that year. The preparatory studies for the conference started in about 1970, which meant that a fifteen-year period lay ahead. Five years of that period have now passed, and the horizon is now only a decade away.

The average population increase during the fifteen-year period had been estimated at about 2.5 percent per annum. World food production, which the FAO Indicative World Plan at the beginning of the 1960s had optimistically estimated would rise by 3.4 percent annually up to 1973, has in fact risen by only 2.6 percent annually. This has been because, among other reasons, irrigation works in a number of countries dependent on irrigation have expanded less rapidly than expected. A more pessimistic view, therefore, is being taken of the growth of food production, which is now expected to be limited to about the same percentage as the rate of population increase. In this case the relationship between population and food production will remain more or less unchanged unless something unexpected occurs.

Today at least 460 million people are considered to be "permanently hungry," which means that their "capacity for living a normal life cannot be realized." Of these, 40 percent are children. Most of them live in rural communities. If the ratio between population increase and food production remains unaltered, the number of permanently hungry persons in the world will have risen to 750 million by 1985.

The extrapolation of current development trends in the conference documents shows very clearly that the situation can rapidly deteriorate. During the coming ten-year period (the period ending in 1985), total grain demand is expected to rise from the present 386 million tons per annum to 630 million tons. During the same period, judging by current trends, production is expected to rise from 370 million tons per annum to 540 million tons per annum. If so, the annual deficit in the developing countries will rise from 16 million tons per annum at present to 85 million tons per annum—a fivefold increase in ten years! If we disregard those developing countries which export large quantities of grain, we find in the nonexporting developing countries a deficit of no less than 100 million tons per annum. This deficit denotes the shortfall in relation to what people in the countries concerned are expected to be capable of buying.

To this deficit must be added the extra food supplies needed to remedy the widespread malnutrition which already exists and which is likely to become far worse. As we have just seen, the number of permanently hungry persons in the world will have passed the 750 million mark by 1985 unless vigorous countermeasures are taken. Another 20 million tons of grain a year would be needed in order to raise the intake of these starving people by 250 calories per capita per day. This brings the annual production deficit up to 120 million tons.

The situation envisaged by these balanced calculations is nothing short of alarming. What can be done to remedy the vast food shortage that will arise in the developing countries in ten years' time? In principle, it would be quite possible to fill the gap with exports from countries—mostly industrialized countries—with grain surpluses, but in terms of grain exports alone this would involve shipments of 80-90 million tons per annum. The financing of transactions of this magnitude would require such fundamental structural changes in payments systems and trade relations that it has not been judged feasible within such a short period of time.

More water—bigger harvests, less starvation

A large-scale, crash operation to raise the food production of the developing countries is therefore essential; otherwise, large areas of the world will be affected within a few years by a more general famine than already exists in several developing countries. It has not been judged a realistic proposition for a significant portion of the expected shortage to be made up by means of transfers in the form of assistance from better-situated countries to starving ones. *Production must, therefore, be raised within the starving countries themselves if disaster is to be avoided.* Action is most needed in those countries, with a view to establishing more reliable production, i.e., production which is less susceptible to inevitable meteorological fluctuations.

It is clear that in order to establish greater and more reliable agricultural production, simultaneous provision will have to be made for a number of different factors: cultivable land, seed, water, fertilizers, plant protection, labor, and expertise. Some of these factors of production can be obtained within a relatively short time, and in the current situation there is consequently a tendency for them to be favored. Short-term factors of this kind include fertilizers and seed disinfection, which attracted a great deal of attention in the Rome documents. But water is usually decisive, shortage of water being a preeminently limiting factor: *water supply is a necessary precondition for justice to be done to other factors of production.* This was realized by authors of the documents for the Rome conference, and a two-stage procedure has, therefore, been conceived for the period ending 1985 with a view to establishing a more reliable water supply for cultivated land. It is proposed, first, to undertake extensive repairs to existing irrigation facilities and, second, to establish new irrigation facilities for land already under cultivation.

There is an enormous need to repair and improve existing irrigation facilities, and measures of this kind would increase food output, above all in the Far East and Southeast Asia. About half the older installations (46 million hectares) are thought to be in need of renovation. This is doubtlessly correct. Irrigation installations in the developing countries are seriously defective. Often there is no water, owing to incorrect planning. For instance, there are great irrigation systems in India which have not received any water from dams for between three and five years. Sometimes the dams and canals are silted up. The renovation of older irrigation facilities must inevitably be accompanied by a review of available water supplies.

Irrigation systems corresponding to 23 million hectares have been proposed for the period ending 1985. If these projects materialize, they will involve a tremendous volume of water consumption. The actual figure is estimated to be more than 250 km^3 per annum, which is thirty-three times the runoff of the Dalälven River, one of the largest rivers in Sweden.

In addition to these measures for raising the productivity of land already under cultivation, it is proposed to increase the world's cultivated acreage from the present 737 million hectares to 890 million hectares in 1985. Most of this increase will have to be effected in thinly populated areas, such as the Amazon basin. In a densely populated country, like India, there is no scope for expansion at all. An increase of these proportions in the cultivated acreage would have considerable hydrological consequences on runoff, erosion, and chemical characteristics of water.

Apart from these measures to raise total food output, efforts are needed to increase the security of production. The reliability of agriculture in the developing countries is greatly impaired by severe climatic fluctuations. Droughts can sometimes persist for several years with disastrous results. Large areas in Africa, for instance, have recently been affected in this way. Measures to guarantee a more regular water supply, such as dam projects or the boring of wells to exploit ground-water resources, can improve the situation.

Improved water supply is, therefore, a vital ingredient in the improvement of world food production and the alleviation of famine. On the other hand, the mere watering of cultivated land is obviously not sufficient in itself. Balanced, optimum production demands a process of interaction between soil, soil conservation, application of water, seed, plant nutrition, etc. But water supply is often fundamental, water being the outstanding deficient factor. The interaction of different factors of production is always in evidence. The failure of the Green Revolution to live up to expectations has been due largely to the impossibility of providing favorable growth conditions for the new high-yielding varieties developed by geneticists and plant breeders. As we noted earlier, the interaction between seed and other factors of production—very often water—has not been satisfactory.

4   *Africa—too wet or too dry?*

Two-thirds of the poorest countries in the world are in Africa

Africa has long been regarded as a continent of low average population density, but the difficulties this continent has in supporting itself have been thrown into sharp relief by the droughts of recent years. Per capita grain production has, in fact, declined from 160 kg per annum between 1961 and 1963 to 130 kg in 1973. Africa contains no less than twenty-five of the thirty-eight poorest countries in the world. Their poverty is dominated by their proximity to the desert, i.e., by a generally dry climate and unfavorable agricultural conditions. A group of researchers from Clark University in the United States has classified these underdeveloped countries into groups according to their geographical location as follows:

1. the countries of the Sahel zone (the Central African Republic, Chad, Mali, Mauretania, Niger, Upper Volta);
2. semiarid countries on the East African coast (Ethiopia, Kenya, Somalia, Sudan, Tanzania);
3. West African coastal countries (Cameroon, Dahomey, Gambia, Guinea, Sierra Leone, Togo); and
4. landlocked countries in East and Southern Africa (Botswana, Burundi, Lesotho, Malawi, Ruanda, Swaziland, Uganda).

The situation is made worse by the fact that fourteen African countries have 85 percent or more of their land area in zones where there is little rainfall. Other adverse natural conditions may occur in the same countries, e.g., poor soils, impassable terrain, long distances to markets, and extremes of temperature. Rainfall is highly capricious, and droughts can persist for several years. There are extensive areas where the soil has been destroyed and is capable of very little production of pasture or crops. The agricultural potential of these areas can never become very high, but at present it is lower than it need be, due to excessive population pressure and mismanagement.

Many of these poor countries are dominated by a single ecosystem, which allows them very little flexibility in land use. Cattle farming is the predominant activity, maximum use being made in this way of an environment which is not only poor but also extremely fragile. Even then, only a very low subsistence level is achieved.

Seen in terms of its potential self-sufficiency in foodstuffs, the continent of Africa can be divided into four main areas:

1. Areas with serious problems concerning resources; these include the Sahel countries and the semiarid zones of East and Southern Africa.
2. Areas ravaged by onchecerciasis and trypanosomiasis. The first of these is a disease which causes blindness and debility and today obstructs the cultivation of large areas of West Africa. The second is an infection, caused by the tse-tse fly, which prevents very large tropical areas (700 Mha) from being brought under cultivation. It also affects cattle.
3. Tropical areas where abundant rainfall creates difficulties for farming.
4. Areas which are ecologically suitable for the production of grain and other crops.

Where and when is there water?

The continent of Africa extends about 30 degrees north and south of the equator and presents a cross section of many of the world's principal climates. No other continent is so symmetrically positioned in relation to the equator. Large areas of Africa are situated in tropical latitudes. Consequently, it is affected more than other continents by the two subtropical belts of high pressure located on either side of the tropical rain forest at the equator; hence, in large areas of Africa the climate is dry and tropical or subtropical.

Africa is often described as one great plateau, and certainly a great deal of its total area is fairly high above sea level. The height of the continent above sea level does a great deal to reduce the (tropical) temperatures of extensive areas. Because of the regular shape of Africa and its lack of sizeable mountain ridges, the climate changes fairly regularly away from the equator. In both directions one finds the same climatic sequence of tropical rain forest climate, semiarid steppe climate, arid desert climate, and, finally, a subtropical Mediterranean climate with dry summers. The term "arid zone" implies that a whole year or more may elapse between falls of rain. The climate is governed to a great extent by the annual north-to-south movement of the rainy tropical belt, which in turn is influenced by the sun. Rainfall is heavy in those areas which at any given moment are located within this rainy belt.

The greatest difference between the northern and southern halves of the continent is caused by the extreme breadth of North Africa, in which the arid zone is extensive. Indeed, the Sahara is the world's largest desert. Its southern counterpart is the much smaller Kalahari. In these desert areas, rainfall is so slight and so irregular that it is pointless to talk about average annual precipitation. The arid Sahara is bordered on two sides by subarid steppe belts. The southernmost of these is the Sudan-Sahel zone, a narrow strip extending continuously from Gambia in the west to the Ethiopian mountain massif in the east. Here a short period of rain lasts between two and four months of the year. This zone was affected recently by a very severe drought, to which reference will be made later.

Needless to say, the high temperatures of the African continent result in high evaporation. Concerning availability of water, it will be recalled from the map on page 3 that most of Africa has a water deficit, i.e., vegetation needs far more water than precipitation supplies. Surpluses occur in two areas only. The larger of these is a triangular zone with its apex a little to the west of Lake Victoria and its base following the west coast between 7°N and 7°S. A great deal of the surplus water in this zone finds its way into the Congo River. The largest water surplus, measured in millimeters per annum, exists along the coast of Cameroon and southern Nigeria. The other surplus area is in West Africa, between Ghana and Guinea. The water surplus nearest the coast in this area is 3,000 mm per annum. Further inland are the sources of the Niger and Senegal rivers.

Water resources are reflected by natural vegetation

Climatic conditions are clearly reflected by natural vegetation. In areas of water surplus *tropical rain forest* occurs. The soil here is heavily leached, because the constant surplus of water causes warm water to seep down into it continuously, dissolving and carrying off the valuable nutrient salts. This makes the soil lateritic and of poor agricultural value. Equatorial soils are extremely deficient in humus compared with ordinary temperate soils, where the humus content may exceed 10 percent. Despite the lack of plant nourishment and humus in these soils, however, natural vegetation is luxuriant. This is a result of nature's own delicate balance, humus and nutrient salts being released by the degradation of fallen or dead plant life and immediately absorbed by the new vegetation which is growing. Farming in these areas is often based on slash-and-burn techniques, whereby the forest is cleared and the land farmed for a year or two until the nutrient salts in the soil have been exhausted and it is time to move on to a new area.

The belts to the north, east, and south of the water-surplus area are characterized, in their natural state, by *savannah*— natural vegetation comprising grass and scattered trees. Trees become more common as one approaches the rain forest zone; towards the desert they give way to thorny bushes. The dry season in the savannah is so long that effective farming is absolutely dependent on irrigation.

Rainfall varies a great deal both in quantity and duration. Precipitation may be 250 mm one year and 1,000 mm the next. Years of meager rainfall spell disaster to cattle farming, which is the main occupation in these zones. Conditions are made still more difficult by the tendency for droughts to occur several years in succession.

Despite its proneness to drought, the tropical savannah is considered potentially capable of contributing a great deal towards better agricultural output for the starving world. The principal drawback is the poor quality of most of its soil, due to the climate and in some instances to human mismanagement. During the dry season, ground moisture is lost by evaporation or by transpiration through the vegetation. A certain amount of brackish groundwater is probably drawn to the surface. This evaporates, leaving its salt content in the soil, which acquires a crusty surface known as "hard pan." During the rainy season the soil is often damaged by erosion and leaching. As a result it becomes unfertile—rich in iron and aluminum hydroxides but deficient in nutrient salts.

Grazing lands are often given very harsh treatment. During the dry season the withered vegetation is burned so that its nutrient salts can be held for the benefit of the next season's growth. Both the soil and the grass are impaired by this procedure, which gradually robs them of nourishment. The inhabitants of these zones tend to be nomads constantly on the move in search of better pastures. They mostly utilize their animals in the living state, milking them and letting their blood but hardly ever slaughtering them. Their cattle are consequently thin and poor, and the herds are much too large for the scanty grazing. Commercial grazing, which has been developed in savannah zones in other parts of the world, e.g., Australia and Latin America, is still rare in Africa, where it is more or less limited to Kenya.

In the desert zones vegetation is very thin. Rainfall is uncommon but does occur on isolated occasions. The only plants growing in these zones are species equipped to make use of the small quantities of available water. The desert may take the form of bare rock exposed by extensive erosion, windswept sand dunes, deep ravines carved by rare flows of water in temporary watercourses, or expanses of cracked clay deposited in the past by a sudden, transitory rush of water.

The rivers of Africa

Climatological conditions are reflected not only by the distribution of vegetation but also by runoff and its distribution over the continent (see map at front of book). The average runoff for the entire continent is 140 mm per annum. This is lower than the average runoff of any other continent. Altogether, runoff totals about 4,000 km³ per annum, which corresponds to four of the flow units referred to in chapter 2, thirty-eight of which were returned to the sea every year by all the continents of the world. Runoff from the continent of Africa is channeled through a number of rivers, the four largest being the Niger and Congo in the west, the Zambesi in the east, and the Nile in the north. The Niger and the Nile are both long rivers, rising in well-watered areas but flowing, on their way to remote estuaries, through arid and semiarid zones in which a great deal of their water is lost by evaporation. Consequently, when they finally reach their estuaries, their water flow is less than when they started.

There are many rivers whose runoff is unknown, because it has not been measured regularly, as is the common practice in the industrialized countries. It is only as a consequence of the International Hydrological Decade organized by the UN Educational, Scientific, and Cultural Organization (UNESCO) that hydrological measurements have begun to be made of many of these rivers (see chapter 8). The Nile, on the other hand, has been hydrologically studied from ancient times, and there were gauging stations along its course thousands of years before the birth of Christ. In its most amply watered stretches, this river carries an annual average of about 3,000 m³ per second, but by the time it reaches its estuary this flow has been reduced to 400 m³ per second.

The central parts of the continent north of the equator drain into Lake Chad, which has no outlet. Runoff into the lake and precipitation over, and evaporation from, its surface closely follow the variations of climate between wet and dry years. Consequently, the water level of Lake Chad fluctuates a great deal. These fluctuations have been recorded ever since 1873. Distinct low-water periods were recorded in 1907-08, 1913-17, and 1972-73. The Cheri River, which flows into the lake, supplied it with 54 km³ water in 1961 but only 17 km³ in the recent, very dry years. The high-water flow, which was 5,200 m³ per second in 1961, was down to between 1,500 and 2,000 m³ per second in the early 1970s. In fact, the drought occurring in these years was so severe that the water level sank to a point where the lake was divided into two separate basins. Heavy evaporation then resulted in a partial drying up of the lake in 1974.

There are large areas of Africa where rivers exist only intermittently. Dry river valleys are occasionally washed by powerful floods of water, sometimes suddenly. On these occasions, the water rushes through from rains in remote areas. Consequently, these rivers are a source of great danger to the inhabitants, who are drawn to dry river beds where it is easier to obtain groundwater infiltrated during the short period when there was water in the river. These sudden floods are also a problem to road builders, who build the road down to the dried-out river bed and up the other side without troubling to build a bridge or viaduct. When the flood comes, it deposits large quantities of mud, making the road temporarily impassable. The mud has to be cleared in order to reopen the road.

As we have just seen, the runoff from the African continent is relatively small compared with that of other continents. On the other hand, the present population of Africa is small enough for the water supply to be fairly abundant when spread out per capita, in fact it is about 12,000 m³ per annum, which is three times the average figure for Europe and twice the figure for Asia.

Where does the population live?

The distribution of the population of Africa can be studied

by means of the pull-out map. This map shows that the dry zones of the north, east, and south are relatively densely populated. The greatest density of population comes in the semiarid zones surrounding the Sahara and in the Nile valley.

The total population of Africa is 344 million, and the UN forecast for the year 2000 indicates a possible 818 million. These trends will, of course, create serious problems in the future. The culmination of the population explosion is still some way off. Owing to the very rapid growth of urban population, the food demand of towns and cities is rising very fast although large areas are inhabited by nomads. In other extensive areas, resources and productivity are being concentrated on export crops. This may inhibit the production of food for the local population, thereby obstructing the achievement of a reasonable level of self-sufficiency.

Viewing the continent of Africa in a global context, it is characterized by a low average density of population and by a fast rate of population growth. Many African countries have as little as one inhabitant per square kilometer (p/km^2), but the population density of some central African areas near the large lakes is well over 100 p/km^2.

The drought-stricken Sahel zone

The Sudano-Sahel zone is the narrow semiarid belt to the south of the Sahara, extending from the northern frontier of Gambia (14°N) and the valley of the Senegal River to the western side of the Ethiopian massif. This zone is characterized by high temperatures and a short rainy season lasting between two and four months in the year. The countries lying within it are Senegal, Gambia, Mali, Niger, Chad, Mauretania, the central portion of the Sudan, and the northern part of Upper Volta. These are the countries which have suffered severe droughts in the past five years. The rainy season begins and ends very abruptly.

As we have already said, the incidence of rainfall is closely bound up with the annual north-south movement of the zone of tropical convergence, i.e., the zone of heavy tropical rainfall. This zone is situated at about 6°N in January and at about 18°N in July. In the higher latitudes the rain falls as sporadic showers, but south of 12°N the probability of rainfall is far greater, and precipitation increases as the equator is approached. The steep decline in precipitation towards the higher latitudes is supposed to be connected with a sensitivity to certain critical weather situations; if these situations coincide, they have very serious effects in the form of extreme drought.

The production capacity of the soil is, of course, closely bound up with the availability of rainfall, as is shown by a report on land becoming desert published recently by Anders Rapp.

Precipitation zones, estimated primary productivity, and cattle raising capacity of the Sahel zone

rain zone	annual rainfall, mm	primary productivity, kg dry matter per hectare	cattle raising capacity, hectare per head of standard cattle (250 kg animals)
Desert side of Sahel zone	100—200	400	10
Typical Sahel	200—400	1 000	3—6
Sudano-Sahel	400—600	1 200—3 000	1,5—6

In large parts of the Sudano-Sahel, the ground is flat and the vegetation consists of strips of steppe vegetation interspersed with ruined soil. The vegetation is in a very delicate state of natural equilibrium, and every disruption of the vegetative cover—for instance, due to excessive grazing—destroys that cover and causes an expansion of soil destruction. The scanty grazing resources of the Sahel zone are utilized by a nomad population. During the rainy season the nomads stay near pools and other sources of surface water. At the beginning of the dry season they move their livestock to tracts near shallow wells, where the groundwater is fairly

71

close to the surface (about 10 meters down). They spend the rest of the dry season near rivers or close to bored wells, where the groundwater lies much deeper (about 100 meters below the surface). The river plains are very valuable pasture, and efforts are being made to counteract the increasing tendency to use them for rice cultivation, because when they are applied to rice growing these areas can be used only for part of the year; during the rest of the year they are left idle and cannot be used for anything.

Farming in the Sahel zone gives meager returns. The method used is known as dry farming, implying cultivation of the land for a succession of years using plant rotations. After each sequence, the land has to lie fallow for a number of years in order to build up its water content. During this period when the soil is left entirely unprotected, it is liable to be eroded by the wind during the dry season and when there is a heavy rainfall, the soil is liable to be washed away.

Because of the increasing pressure of population, herds have grown too large and the poor soil has been overexploited. Both these circumstances are conducive to heavy destruction of the soil. Dry years inflict particularly serious damage to the soil, ultimately changing it to desert. The gradual expansion of the deserts is now thought to be partly due to human activity. Conversion to desert occurs when the vegetation cover is reduced below a certain critical limit corresponding to what is needed to protect the soil against rapid erosion by wind and water. Formerly, transition to desert was interpreted as a slow, gradual advance of the desert front. This, in turn, led to the idea of planting belts of trees to stop the sand from spreading further south. Plans have, in fact, been evolved for a forest belt of this kind along the fifteenth parallel from the bend of the Niger river to Lake Chad. Today, however, this idea is thought to have been founded on a misinterpretation, since it has now been discovered that conversion to desert is a local process which can begin in any sensitive dry area as soon as the protective cover of vegetation is destroyed by grazing or cultivation.

Widespread wind erosion in this zone results in great clouds of dust being carried across the Atlantic and into the

Nile valley. On the island of Barbados, in the West Indies, a total transfer of 30 million tons in the form of dust clouds was measured within the space of three months during 1969. Thus, every year Africa loses enormous amounts of soil, particularly as a result of land becoming desert.

As mentioned earlier, it is a characteristic of the semiarid zones that their rainfall can fluctuate considerably from one year to another. It is also common for several dry years to follow in succession. As everybody who owns a TV set will remember, the Sahel zone suffered a severe drought between 1968 and 1973, but there have been earlier droughts. Between 1907 and 1915, there was a drought which was just as severe, although perhaps less widespread. Between 1910 and 1914, the Senegal and Upper Niger rivers had lower river discharge than between 1968 and 1972. Statistical analysis of the latest drought has indicated that it was no worse than is to be expected roughly once every fifty years. Its impact was severely felt because a population increase had led to a heavy expansion of the stock of cattle, following the abundant rains between 1950 and 1963.

The extent of the disaster is not easily quantified. The joint committee set up by the drought-stricken countries estimated that about four million head of cattle were lost in the six West African countries affected. The harvest deficit was estimated at 0.850 million tons. Far more serious, however, was the immeasurable damage inflicted on the natural environment, which among other things led to large areas becoming desert. On the other hand, it was thought that few human beings starved to death. Food supplies were meager, however, and the famine was so serious that the population became debilitated. It will take a long time to restore their work capacity. The surviving cattle were also weakened, and this will affect their reproductive capacity and yield for a long time to come.

Engineering the economic development of the countries of the Sahel zone will be no easy task. Politicians now have to face a population which is no longer prepared to accept the caprices of its climate. The drought of 1913 was also severe, but the inhabitants then were of a more patient disposition;

they accepted the alternation of good and bad years, and they spoke Biblically of the fat and the lean kine. Today we are confronted by a fundamental change that is forcing the authorities to act with a greater sense of purpose. Every reasonable measure, therefore, must now be taken to stabilize the living conditions of the population. Climatic conditions alone can no longer be permitted to govern agriculture. This means that the irrigated acreage will have to be increased. In other words, the focus of political attention in these countries is on problems of water supply. Preparations are being made for penetrating studies of water supply problems, and it is realized that various measures will have to be taken in order to give agriculture the greatest possible protection from the effects of constant fluctuations of climate. The prime concern is with river water as a source of public supply and irrigation.

Planning for safer cattle farming is a more complex task, with the result that plans are delayed. For climatic reasons, grazing is not available for several months of the year, during which cattle have to be fed in some other way. Before the drought, efforts were being made to raise yields by protecting pasture, providing better health services for the cattle, and increasing the number of water holes. Since the drought, it has become clear that this was not enough. The effects of an excessive density of watering places can be seen from the figure on page 77.

It is vitally important in this zone for effective use to be made of the water available both in the rivers and in the ground. As things stand today, much precious water is left unused and allowed to flow into the sea. Dams will have to be built to store the water from the rainy season, and wells will have to be bored down to the groundwater. Another important requirement is the improvement of grazing lands by the introduction of drought-resistant plant species and by stricter control of herd sizes. A third essential requirement is for the adaptibility and yield of the cattle to be improved by reducing the size of herds and improving the breed.

74

North Africa — once the granary of Rome

On the northern edge of the Sahara, the arid zone extends almost to the coast. The only fertile land here is a narrow strip with a semiarid climate or, in the extreme north—especially on the northern slopes of the Atlas Mountains—a Mediterranean climate. Water supplies are at their worst in Morocco and Tunisia, the latter once the granary of Rome. The natural vegetation of North Africa covers 10-80 percent of the area and takes the form of a bushy steppe characterized by perennial species between 30 and 60 cm high. Vegetation in the desert zone is mostly confined to low-lying areas around oases and to the sporadically watered river valleys or wadis.

The arid parts of this zone are inhabited by about twelve million people, roughly one million of whom are nomads. The majority live, directly or indirectly, by agriculture and animal breeding. The animals are sheep, goats, donkeys, beef cattle, and camels—about thirty million altogether, which is more than 2.5 times as many as the grazing potential of the land can support. The most widely cultivated crops are wheat and barley, but yields are poor, about 250-300 kg per hectare. Each family has an average of five hectares to live on; this is below the subsistence minimum. Orchards of olive, almond, fig, and apricot trees cover about 1.5 mega-hectares (Mha), about one-third of the area being irrigated land on which citrus fruits and date palms are also cultivated.

Soil destruction is a serious problem in this zone. The vegetation is gradually disappearing, and nature has great difficulty in repairing damage once it has occurred. In the driest areas, the damage is irreparable. For instance, the tracks made by German, French, and British tanks in Libya and southern Tunisia during the Second World War are still clearly visible today.

Further conversion of land to desert is being caused by the destruction of vegetation resulting from removal of the natural vegetation, bad cultivation, clearance of forests for fuel, excessive grazing by oversized herds of cattle, and the burning of grazing lands, although this last-mentioned practice is more common south of the Sahara.

There have long been consecutive periods of drought in this zone; they are a characteristic feature of the prevailing climate. But before man started to treat nature so roughly, the natural vegetation was in a state of equilibrium with the conditions of growth and climate in the zone, with the result that the vegetation was able to recover after several years of intense drought. This recuperative capacity has now been lost, due to the maltreatment of soil resulting from human folly.

The adoption of modern ploughing methods is thought to have made a substantial contribution to the process of destruction. The new plough penetrates more deeply into the soil and destroys the perennial vegetation. Moreover, cultivation methods are used whereby the soil is left bare for several months in the year, with the result that, here as in the Sahel zone, it is eroded by wind and water. Wind erosion is said to remove a millimeter of top soil every month, and water erosion removes roughly the same amount in a year. In one part of Libya where the annual precipitation rate is

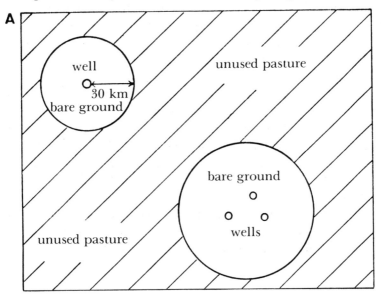

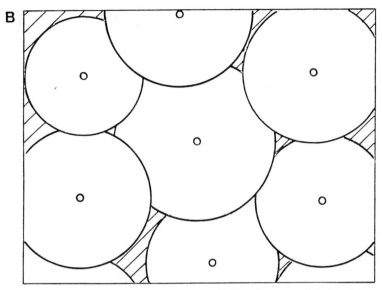

B

If wells are sited too close together, pasture is liable to be overexploited in dry years. The picture on p. 76 shows the original situation at the end of the dry season. The size of the herd is limited by the grazing available during the dry season. A small population can survive by grazing its cattle. Picture this page illustrates the situation after the completion of a well-drilling project. Much bigger herds and a much bigger population can be provided for in normal years, but the system breaks down in an extremely dry year, because the grazing is then exhausted before the next rainy season begins. After Rapp.

between 150 and 250 mm, within no more than the past ten or fifteen years, the desert has expanded to such an extent that 40,000 hectares of sand dunes have developed as a result of this careless ploughing.

This pattern of development is all the more lamentable when one recalls how the soil of North Africa was once the granary of Rome. It is worth noting that the climate is not thought to have been more favorable in Roman times. Ecologically speaking, therefore, the area should still be able to produce quite abundant crops if the population were only to devote as much attention to soil and water conservation as was shown under the Romans. Rainfall is adequate, and the soil is suitable for cultivation in those places which have not yet been reached by the ongoing process of soil destruction. The importance of the area to the logistics of ancient Rome is attributed, not to any superiority of climate compared with other areas, but among other things to a plentiful supply of cheap labor.

Groundwater resources beneath the Sahara

People in the Arab countries are very much aware of the importance of water to general development. Basically, there are four ways of obtaining water. Precipitation, which falls in winter and generally exceeds 400 mm per annum, is sufficient to sustain a wheat harvest in North Africa. South of the Sahara, where precipitation falls during the summer and where its effect is reduced by heavy evaporation losses, larger quantities are needed for a single harvest. Rivers provide a certain amount of surface water. The Nile is by far the most important source of water supply and sustains practically the entire population of Egypt. People living in dry areas without any life-giving rivers near at hand are completely dependent on groundwater, which to them is the most important of all natural assets. The fourth way of obtaining water is the unconventional method of seawater desalinization, but this is only possible in certain highly favorable conditions.

The value of groundwater has long been known in these dry countries. The technique of capturing it in the mountain areas, where it was formed by more generous rains, and of taking it from there through subterranean aqueducts down to the plains had already been developed several thousand years before the Christian era. These conduits were dug from evenly spaced wells joined by subterranean channels. The tunnels are easily discovered from the air, because they are marked by long rows of characteristic sandhills. There are many different names for these subterranean aqueducts, e.g. foggara, kharez, and khanat, through which water flows by gravity. The very first of these tunnels was probably made in Persia, whence the technique spread to the Mediterranean, where examples are to be found in Greece and Spain. Many of the aqueducts which still serve the city of Rome are of a similar type.

78

Far below large areas of the dry and inhospitable sand and rock of the Sahara lie vast quantities of groundwater. A great deal of the groundwater beneath the Sahara and other African deserts is fossil water. It has lain below the ground for several tens of thousands of years and probably originated with the copious rains that fell in this zone at the beginning of our Ice Age. Some of the groundwater of the Sahara, however, may be renewable, and the aquifer is replenished by rainfall on the southern slopes of the Atlas Mountains, from which it descends to a great depth below the desert. Groundwater occurs in several strata, fed by rainwater from various remote mountain areas where the rainfall is, or used to be, sufficient for the formation of groundwater (see figure, p. 80). Owing to the difference in level between the infiltration area and the deep aquifers in the desert, the groundwater is under artesian pressure and is capable of forcing its way upwards through fissures to form springs, around which natural oases have developed. Man has then taken the opportunity to dig channels from the oases to irrigate fields and plantations of trees with the spring water. In some areas the groundwater has been formed by seepages of river water and is located quite close to the ground surface.

Some Arab countries are in a position to obtain water by desalinization. These countries have the advantage of cheap sources of energy from their own oil wells, as well as from the natural gas, which is not exploited but discharged into the atmosphere as a waste product. Desalinization is more feasible in these countries than in most others because in these cases costs are not insurmountable. However, desalinization does involve heavy investment costs and is, therefore, considered suitable primarily as a means of supplying water to coastal communities and industries. It is not yet cheap enough to be economically viable for irrigation purposes.

In the steppes and deserts of North Africa, water for animals used to be fetched from dug wells, some of which were deep. Today a great many new wells are being drilled to pump water from the aquifers deep below the Sahara. There are certain problems, however. This groundwater may

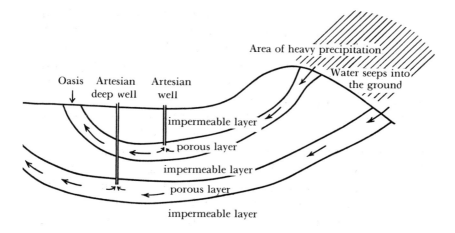

Beneath the desert there may be several strata of groundwater aquifers. These are fed with rainwater from a remote high mountain area. The groundwater is trapped between more impermeable layers and is under pressure (artesian). The rainwater may have accumulated a very long time ago.

contain large quantities of salt—a memento of its long journey through various geological formations—and be corrosive. Extra care must therefore be taken to insure maintenance of pipes and pumps, because all metal components are attacked by the water.

Natural and artificial oases

Modern well-drilling techniques have opened up new opportunities for irrigating large, newly cultivated areas and for making better use of grazing facilities for cattle. On the other hand, improved water supply is liable to encourage the maintenance of excessively large herds, which in turn results in overgrazing and land becoming desert. Well-drilling technology is also used to create oases for the cultivation of new areas. Seen from the air, these oases resemble dark circles in the light sand. The circles are about 100 hectares in area and are watered by pipes radiating from the well in the center.

Natural oases are usually to be found in hollows where artesian groundwater from water-bearing formations has forced its way to the surface. If oases of this kind were to be cultivated too intensively, however, an excessive amount of salts precipitated by the groundwater would accumulate in the soil as a result of irrigation. This would result in salinization, which would ultimately render the soil completely barren. For this reason, efforts are usually made, when establishing new oases, to lead the groundwater to a point in the terrain which is fairly high above the lowest point of the depression. This makes it easier for the salts to be flushed out with surplus water when the need arises. The salt water can then run down into the depression, where it eventually forms salt deposits.

One thing which must always be borne in mind is that as more and more artesian water is extracted for irrigation, the pressure gradually declines, with the result that extraction becomes progressively more difficult and more expensive. Fossil water is a nonrenewable resource, and eventually the level will sink to a point where the expense of boring deeper wells becomes prohibitive. The governments of such countries will therefore encounter difficulties in the future insofar as oasis development is based on a natural resource which will become either more and more inaccessible or eventually be exhausted. In the long term, the only reliable groundwater is that which is formed in present-day climatic conditions.

Egypt—a product of the life-giving Nile

Practically the whole of Egypt comes within the arid zone, and several years may pass between rainfalls. Only the northern coastal zone is situated within the semiarid zone, and even there precipitation is not more than 150 mm per annum. This precipitation is unpredictable. The area has a shallow water table from which groundwater is raised by means of wind-driven pumps. More than a thousand of these pumps have been constructed in the past ten years.

Egypt's most important water resources are the Nile and

the richly watered Nubian Sandstone. The groundwater in the Nubian Sandstone, which extends beneath a considerable area of the country, is a very important source of supply. The sandstone is so porous that the water can readily percolate through it. Its maximum thickness is 1,400 meters, and it is said to transport 5 million m³ daily. In the area west of the Nile, with its many depressions, the groundwater flows into a number of oases. This groundwater may possibly be fossil water.

The Nile is the paramount source of water supply. From time immemorial it has been used for irrigation, and without it life in this predominantly desert area would be impossible. The Nile is one of the world's great alien rivers, "alien" being the term used for a river which rises in an area of more ample rainfall. The Nile rises near the Equator (the White Nile) and in Ethiopia (the Blue Nile). As early as 5000 B.C., King Menes dammed up the waters of the Nile with banks of clay to retain the flood water in low-lying areas. The pharaohs went further and built irrigation channels. By about 1000 B.C. the shadoof, a type of water pump, was in general use as a means of lifting water from the river to irrigation channels higher up. Using a bucket and balancing weight on a pivoted pole, one man could lift enough water to irrigate 0.1 hectare per day. A later invention was the Archimedian screw, a spiral inside a close fitting cylinder which could lift water from the river. The saqia, which appeared later still, is a large wooden wheel in which clay pots are fastened. With a buffalo to drive this wheel, a peasant could now irrigate two hectares daily. The saqia is still in general use today (see figure on the following page).

The river discharge of the Nile is 84 km³ per annum (about 3,000 m³ per second) in the upper part of Egypt, but the natural seasonal variations are such that the low flow was not even sufficient for the irrigation practiced in Egypt at the turn of the century. A dam was built at Aswan in 1920 to retain some of the water from the high-water floods. This dam was enlarged ten years later to increase its storage capacity, and a further enlargement was made in 1933.

The mean river-discharge of the Nile also varies consid-

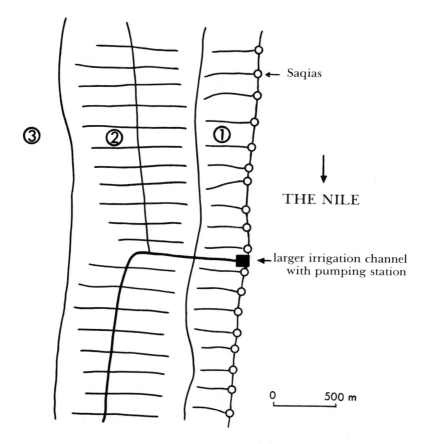

③   ②   ①

← Saqias

↓

THE NILE

←larger irrigation channel
with pumping station

0   500 m

The irrigation channels nearest the river in the Nile valley are supplied with water by separate saqias—wooden wheels with clay pots around their circumference. The channels further inland are supplied with water from a pumping station near the shore.

erably from year to year, due to the generally capricious climatic conditions of the African continent. In recent years it has varied between 42 and 150 km³ per annum. Consequently, the amount of river discharge at the estuary also varies from year to year. In some years the river has run dry; in others it has carried twice the lowest river flow at Aswan. To even out these fluctuations, another Aswan Dam has been built—this time at a new point on the river. People all over the world have been able to watch the growth of the

High Dam on their television screens. It is 111 meters high, and its reservoir, Lake Nasser, is large enough to hold practically all water, from years of heavy river flow to dry years. Lake Nasser has been gauged, according to the average river flow for the past sixty years, at 84 km³ per annum. The water of the Nile is divided between Egypt and the Sudan on the following terms:

	former agreement 1949	new agreement
Egypt	48	55,5
Sudan	4	18,5
evaporation losses	} 32	10
surplus		0
	84	84

Egypt has a serious population problem. Two people now have to live on the area which supported one person at the turn of the century. The recent wars with Israel have slowed down developments, and people are now taking part in hunger marches to underline the gravity of the situation. A solution of the population problem depends on the advanced development, care, and effective utilization of the water of the Nile and of groundwater resources in the Delta and in the Nubian Sandstone. Desalinization of seawater is envisaged as a last resort for irrigating the coastal areas.

Bold plans which have been drawn up for the future include a fuller utilization of the waters of the Nile. This is an international enterprise, because the Nile passes through several countries. There are plans for turning Lake Victoria into a great reservoir to be regulated in such a way as to even out the discharge of the Victoria Nile, which is the outlet of Lake Victoria, between dry years and years of abundant rainfall. The water will then be used for the generation of electricity in Uganda. At the same time, over-year storage of the White Nile is to be established in Lake Albert, where the runoff into Sudan and Egypt will be brought under control.

A regulator for the control of Lake Kyoga is to be established between Lake Victoria and Lake Albert. Downstream of Lake Albert, the White Nile, which now joins the Victoria Nile, passes through a large swamp area, the Sudd, where a great deal of water is lost through evaporation and transpiration from the abundant marsh vegetation. It is planned to divert the Nile round this area by a canal, the Jonglei Canal.

The Blue Nile is a tributary from Ethiopia. Its flow is to be regulated in Lake Tana in Ethiopia, where over-year storage is also to be made possible. Egypt hopes as a result of all these control measures to be able to use an additional 9 km³ of water from the Nile annually. This would make it possible to increase the cultivated acreage by 1.5 Mha.

Irrigation has made the whole of the Nile valley into an oasis which contrasts so sharply with the neighboring desert that it is literally possible to stand with one foot in the desert and the other in the oasis. Primitive arrangements for raising the flood water make it possible to irrigate a strip about 450 meters wide. Using modern diesel pumps this can be increased to a far wider strip of land on both sides of the river (see figure, page 84).

From time immemorial the many oases on the western side of the Nile have been watered with artesian water from the Nubian Sandstone. This chain of oases is now scheduled for a project called the New Valley, covering an area of 90,000 km². Under the project, large areas are to be irrigated with some of the water from the various control measures included in the Upper Nile project. The intention is that water will be brought from Aswan along a 40 km channel, from which it will flow by gravity to the fields. The possibility of basing irrigation on groundwater is also being considered, but river water has been found to constitute a more economical proposition in the long run.

East Africa is also dry

Tanzania lies between the Indian Ocean and Lake Victoria and between the equator and about 10° south. Its climate presents the seasonal variations between dry and rainy periods which are so typical of savannah regions. The water balance is negative in that potential evaporation, which amounts to 2,000 - 2,500 mm per annum, greatly exceeds precipitation. Typical precipitation rates are 500 - 750 mm per annum in central Tanzania and 750 - 1,250 mm per annum in the eastern and western regions. Precipitation varies considerably during the course of the year, but even in the rainy season it is less than 150 mm per month in many parts of the country. The very dry season can last up to seven months, but its duration varies from one region to another.

As in other parts of Africa, there is a great deal of variation from year to year. Farming does not derive much benefit from years of heavy rainfall, because the surplus runs off in the form of heavy floods, when the soil becomes saturated and unable to absorb more water. The extremely dry periods limit cultivation, and areas with less than 750 mm precipitation per annum are considered of marginal importance for agricultural purposes. Only in 20 percent of the area of the country is this condition satisfied with 90 percent certainty, i.e., with not more than one excessively dry year in ten. Thus, farming in Tanzania operates with very narrow margins, and the country is in great need of irrigation.

The development of irrigation facilities is progressing very slowly. There is no doubt that water supply is one of the most crucial factors connected with the improvement of living conditions and securing the future of economic development in East Africa. The aim is for the entire population to be given a regular supply of drinking water by 1991, and great efforts are being made to achieve this by East African standards. A great deal of the development program is made possible by Swedish financial and technical assistance, focusing above all on rural development. In 1968 only 10 percent of the rural population and 60 percent of the urban population had access to running water.

The establishment of a main water supply in the countryside has a number of favorable effects, both direct and indirect. It improves the state of health of the population. It improves productivity, because the women, who spent up to six hours of every day fetching water, can now occupy themselves with other jobs. Village democracy—ujamaa—develops and self-reliance increases, which is an important objective in Tanzania. Modernization is changing attitudes, and by a greater acceptance of technology, living standards are being improved.

Little is known about the replenishment of groundwater. There are isolated natural sources of limited size. The isolated mountains which rise above the savannah may be the areas which give rise to the recharge, precipitation over such mountains (and hills) being heavier than in the surrounding plain. However, the amount of precipitation seeping down into the groundwater reservoirs cannot be large. Measurements taken outside Nairobi over a period of sixteen years indicate that not more than 2-3 percent of the precipitation reached the groundwater. This infiltration occurred as a result of two exceptionally rainy periods; periods of normal precipitation are incapable of making any contribution to the groundwater reserve.

Here, as elsewhere, a country with heavy fluctuations between dry and rainy periods is faced with the risk of erosion. Towards the end of the dry periods the soil is so exposed that the heavy rains at the beginning of the rainy season have a devastating effect. Extremely heavy rainfall may produce disastrous landslides in cultivated mountain slopes. To solve this erosion problem, farming methods have to be adapted to natural conditions. Agricultural planning must, of course, be based on a detailed knowledge of hydrological processes and soil stratification in the area.

Earth concentrations of 10 g/liter have been measured in floodwater. It is not surprising therefore that sedimentation is a serious problem in dams and reservoirs. There have been cases of large dams silting up completely after only fifteen years. Sedimentation, therefore, presents particular economic problems where the planning of surface water reservoirs is concerned. In recent years, consideration has been given the possibility of using silted reservoirs for other purposes, such as cultivation.

The way to the future

In this chapter a description has been given of the water problems of some of the semiarid and arid areas of North Africa. Much the same conditions apply, of course, in the corresponding parts of the southern half of the continent. The problems of the tropical zone, with its copious rainfall, are of an essentially different kind and bear a close resemblance to the problems of the Amazon basin (to which reference will be made in chapter 6).

According to the documents of the UN Food Conference in Rome, the most important requirement where Africa is concerned is for effective use of existing water resources through the construction of dams (mostly small earth dams) and the drilling of wells. Today much precious water is lost to the ocean. The next step is to improve grazing lands by introducing hardy plant species and by adjusting herd sizes. Efforts will then have to be made to evolve a better adapted and more productive breed of cattle, in the short run by thinning out the existing types and numbers and on a more long-term basis through research programs aimed at genetic improvements. An assault must be made on the waterborne diseases now hindering the utilization of river valleys, and also upon the vast domains of the tse-tse fly. The agricultural technology available at present is far too limited to permit the development of agricultural output which is needed today. Technical modernization is essential as a means of improving traditional crops and raising agricultural capacity to self-sufficiency level.

FAO does not believe it is realistic, for the period ending in 1985, to aim at repairing more than about 1 Mha of the irrigation facilities presently out of action and establishing about 1 Mha more in the form of new facilities. On the other hand, some 35 Mha of new land will have to be brought under the plough within the next ten years in order to avert the impending disaster. Where Africa is concerned, one must always be mindful of the fluctuating weather conditions which are a feature of the natural history of the continent and which must, therefore, be accepted in this part of the world. The aim must be to alleviate the effects of these fluctuations by using wells, dams, irrigation, and drainage to control the available supply of water. Forecasting and warning services are also needed, and emergency stocks of grain will have to be accumulated on a scale sufficient to meet requirements coming after periods of extreme rainfall fluctuations.

Natural conditions in Africa are subject to both short-term and long-term change. There has been a long-term change towards drier climatic conditions, as witness the cave paintings in the Sahara and the abundance of fossil groundwater. Short-term climatic trends are less readily discernible. On the other hand, human activity plays an important part in this perspective: the extension of deserts, for instance, can be attributed to the over-exploitation of sensitive soil. Increasing extraction of groundwater may also contribute to a gradual dessication.

Large areas of arid and semiarid Africa now seem to be basing their social development on supplies of groundwater which may be of fossil origin to a greater extent than was previously supposed. Age determinations recently undertaken on water from several of the deep-seated groundwater reservoirs indicate that the water infiltrated several tens of thousands of years ago. This water is now reaching the surface in oases because it is under pressure, but the pressure is steadily declining. The Nubian Sandstone, for instance, contains an abundance of water but probably is not being replenished. It is important to realize that permanent communities cannot be established on the basis of fossil groundwater.

5

Asia—a densely populated continent

Vast areas of Asia have a water deficit

Asia covers about one-third of the earth's surface but has nearly two-thirds of its population. The continent incorporates many different kinds of topography. The central areas are made up of plateaus and high mountain ranges. Great deserts extend in a wide strip from the ever-warm deserts of the Arabian peninsula northeastwards to the Gobi in Mongolia, where the winters are very cold. These desert areas are mostly inhabited by nomads who, like their counterparts in Africa, wander in search of water and pasture for their livestock. Northern Asia has extensive areas of tundra and coniferous forests. Further south, there is a steppe zone of grasslands, and in the very south lies the hot and rainy equatorial zone with its steaming jungles.

As we are mainly concerned in this book with the developing countries, we focus our attention on the southern half of Asia. As can be seen from the map on page 3, this part of Asia figures largely among the water-deficit areas of the world. Thus, rainfall is not sufficient for the type of vegetation which temperature conditions permit. This applies to the entire western part of southern Asia. India and Indonesia are the only places with a water surplus.

Apart from its mountainous areas, Southern Asia has a hot climate all the year round. The year is divided into a rainy season and a dry season. The rains last from June till October, with daily cloudbursts in some places. Cherrapunji in the north of India receives more than 10,000 mm (10 meters) of rain every year. The regular alternation of rainy and dry periods is connected with the monsoon winds, which are the main factor governing the climate of Asia. During winter, a dry, cold wind blows from Central Asia towards the southern and eastern parts of the continent. In summer, the wind blows in the opposite direction, carrying moist, rain-laden air over the land areas. The reverse applies in Southwest Asia, where the summers are long and hot and the winters mild. In some areas winter is the rainy part of the year, during which crops can be cultivated without irrigation.

Most of the rivers of Asia rise in the mountain areas of Central Asia, whence they radiate—the Ob, Yenisey, and Lena northwards to the Arctic Ocean; the Indus, Ganges, Brahmaputra, and Mekong southwards; the Yangtse-Kiang and Yellow River eastwards. Millions and millions of people inhabit the warm, fertile valleys of these rivers.

Needless to say, climate has a crucial effect on people's living conditions. In Burma, for example, which is a warm country with heavy rainfall, inundations are a common event during the rainy season. Burman houses are usually built on piles to keep them above the flood water. The climate is ideal for rice growing. Afghanistan, by contrast, is a dry, mountainous country. Agriculture is confined to river valleys and to cases where there is water available for irrigation. In South and East Asia, farming practices are adapted to the monsoon winds.

Asia is very densely populated indeed

The total population of Asia is more than 2 billion, which is about 60 percent of the population of the earth. Most of these 2 billion people live in South and East Asia. China and India are the two most heavily populated countries with 700 and 500 million inhabitants respectively. South and East Asia are characterized by great density of population and a high rate of population growth. The valley of the Ganges, the area surrounding the Lower Brahmaputra and large areas of China, has more than 200 inhabitants per km^2. Undernourishment is widespread in large areas of Asia, and in India it could be described as commonplace.

In this chapter we shall concentrate on the water problems

of some of the heavily populated countries of South and East Asia. All these have abundant precipitation, confined to part of the year, and dense populations. All cultivable land is already under the plough, and the only possible way of improving agricultural output is to raise yields. This means increasing the number of harvests by irrigating during that part of the year when there is no rainfall but the temperature is high enough for crops to grow. Another problem is that the monsoon is irregular and may fail to arrive. If it comes late in the year, the rainy season may be too short for the crops to have time to ripen. Some areas are so densely populated that a single monsoon failure spells immediate disaster and widespread famine. Alternately, the monsoon may be overabundant, giving rise to heavy inundations which carry away the soil or ruin standing crops.

We now turn to a more detailed discussion of the problems of India, Bangladesh, and China. Our reason for choosing these countries in preference to the countries of the Near East is that the problems of the latter, as far as water supply is concerned, closely resemble those of the dry countries of Africa, to which we paid particular attention in the previous chapter. In the Near East, for example, the land is fed by the great twin rivers, Tigris and Euphrates. In many places there are groundwater deposits from which, as in Africa, water is collected by khanats. Along the shores of the Persian Gulf are a number of oil-rich countries where desalinization of seawater is economically feasible. Kuwait, for example, which until 1946 was mainly populated by nomads and oasis communities, now derives practically the whole of its water supply from the desalinization of seawater.

India—at the mercy of the monsoon

India is a continent in its own right, larger than Western Europe. The country is a union of twenty-one federated states and nine centrally governed territories. It has the same disparity of languages, ethnic groups, religions, and geographical subdivisions as Europe, and it has not advanced very much further than Europe along the path of self-generated political integration. India has 550 million inhabitants, i.e., one-sixth of the earth's population. Of these, 70 percent are dependent on agriculture for their livelihood. The population of India is growing by about 14 million every year. Fifty-five percent of the total area of the country is cultivable, and agriculture accounts for half the national income. Climate, geology, topography, soil conditions, and vegetation all vary a great deal; India has lofty mountain ranges, undulating hills, high plateaus, and rolling plains. Savannah and steppe are the natural vegetation of large areas of the peninsula.

South Asia derives the greater part of its precipitation from the southwest monsoon, which blows from the Indian Ocean. This monsoon is made up of two moisture currents. One, coming from the Arabian Sea, strikes the mountain ridge of the Western Ghats along the west coast of India, discharging heavy amounts of rain in the process. The other comes in over the Bay of Bengal, where it veers northwest and becomes a southeast air current sweeping over the lowlands of northern India. Both these air currents carry large quantities of moisture but they discharge only 20 percent of their moisture content on India. Spread out over the entire area of the country, this is equivalent to an average annual precipitation of 1,100 mm, making 3,700 km^3 in all. About a third of this precipitation evaporates, and about 1,700 km^3 return to the sea through the rivers. It is estimated that the remaining 20 percent or 790 km^3 seep into the ground and recharge deep-seated groundwater reservoirs. Of this amount 270 km^3 are thought to be available. The densely populated valleys of the Ganges and Brahmaputra are particularly well endowed with groundwater. Central India is a primary plateau of rocks similar to those underlying large areas of Sweden and Finland. This rock is usually well-fissured, especially in the uppermost 30 meters.

India's precipitation is unevenly distributed. In the eastern parts of the Himalayas and along the mountain range of the west coast it amounts to 4,000 mm per annum. In the east of the country, local precipitation can be as much as 10 meters per annum in parts of Assam. Central and Southern India, on the other hand, lie in the rain shadow of the Ghats and receive less than 600 mm per annum, which is roughly the same precipitation rate as southeast Sweden. The driest areas are the northwestern states of Rajastan, with its Thar desert, and Gujarat, north of Bombay, where precipitation is less than 100 mm per annum. Ninety percent of India's rainfall falls during the short rainy season between June and September.

The rivers drain the entire area of the country except for the desert area of Rajastan, and for the most part run east and west. The following is a summary of India's resources of river water (cf. map, p. 101):

Ganges—Brahmaputra	876 km³/yr
Indus (eastern tributaries)	40 km³/yr
Eastward-flowing rivers in the Indian subcontinent (Mahanadi, Godavari, Krishna, Cauvery, etc.)	414 km³/yr
Westward-flowing rivers in the Indian subcontinent (Tapi, Marmada, etc.)	308 km³/yr
Total	1,638 km³/yr

It is stressed that these figures are not reliable, because it is only recently that gauging has been undertaken on any considerable scale. There are two kinds of river: snow-fed, giving use to perennial floods in the north and northwest, and monsoon-fed, associated with intermittent floods in central and southern India, where rivers regularly dry up during the dry season.

On account of its tropical climate, the irregularity of the monsoons and their limitation to a few months of the year, India is greatly dependent on irrigation for stable and successful agriculture. Without irrigation, farming in India would be a gamble with the forces of nature. The great plains of the Indus, Ganges, and Brahmaputra have been farmed for at least 6,000 years. Irrigation is also a very ancient science, and there are many remains of prehistoric constructions. Some installations from historic but remote times are still in use today. Irrigation received a stimulus in the mid-19th century, but the partition of the subcontinent, in 1947, gave most of the irrigated areas to West Pakistan. India acquired land areas where rainfall was highly capricious. The irrigated acreage at that time amounted to some 20 Mha, equalling about 20 percent of the total cultivable area. A massive development program was launched which gave top priority to the development of water resources. The program of planned management recently completed its fourth five-year planning period and the irrigation acreage in 1947 has now been at least doubled. Altogether, 22 Mha are now provided with large- or medium-sized irrigation works and an equally large area provided with small-scale works. Water irrigation is divided more or less equally, from groundwater, surface water distributed by state-owned canals, surface water distributed through privately-owned canals, and water from rainwater cisterns.

Groundwater is most important for short-term planning

The Green Revolution came to India in the 1960s. It first gathered speed on the fertile plains of the northwest and south, where groundwater was readily available for the necessary irrigation. Irrigation is, in fact, essential for the successful cultivation of the new high-yield plant varieties and also for the raising of several crops per year. Water has to be supplied at the right time and in the right quantities. After the severe drought of 1965-67 came a veritable explosion of groundwater exploitation and of agricultural development in general. As we saw in chapter 3, groundwater offers the farmer great advantages—it is near at hand and he has only to push the button to start a pump when his fields need watering. The extraction of groundwater is within the capabilities of ordinary people; wells can be dug relatively quickly, and there are cheap pumps on the market. The water becomes available as soon as the well has been constructed, and the very first harvest usually covers the investment cost. This development has greatly enhanced the self-reliance of the population, which is an extremely important development factor. There is a world of difference between the attitudes and mental activity of the farmer who must wait passively for the rains to come, or for somebody a long way away to set the water flowing through the state-owned canals, and the farmer who knows that he can turn on the water as, and when, he sees fit to do so.

In the great river plains, groundwater is readily available close to the ground surface, and adequate wells can be dug with a spade. In the highlands, irrigation from open mountain wells is a long-established practice. In the Coimbatore district of the southernmost state of Tamil Nadu, for instance, there are 100,000 open wells and as many small-scale irrigation units. These walls are of impressive dimensions— often more than 50 m^2 across and 30 meters deep. During the severe drought of 1877-78, wells of this kind provided a never-failing water supply. Oxen have traditionally been used to draw up the water, but in recent years, as the countryside has become electrified, animal power has been superseded by the electric pump. This has resulted in the extraction of larger quantities and, consequently, in a falling water table and the need to deepen wells. In the Coimbatore district alone, well deepening has involved the excavation and removal of 30 mm^3 of rock since the 1930s— the equivalent of five years' output of iron ore in Sweden!

There is great confidence in India in the potentialities of continued groundwater exploitation. As we have just seen, however, rapidly increasing groundwater extraction is liable to outstrip the infiltration of rainwater. Declining water tables show that this is actually happening. In the Coimbatore district, for example, the open wells are now being supplemented by large numbers of new wells drilled to greater depths. The Mission of the Church of Sweden and the

96

Swedish Missionary Society are playing an active part in this work, but the Royal Swedish Institute of Technology and the Swedish International Development Authority are now investigating the potential groundwater extraction capacity of the area and communicating Swedish technological experience in the utilization of groundwater from bedrock.

A number of major projects have been completed to provide water for irrigation. Constructions for irrigation purposes have developed from simple diversion dams placed across the river bed to the present-day gate dams. The 226-meter-high Bhakra Dam on one of the tributaries of the Indus ranks among the largest concrete dams in the world. The pride of the country is the Nagarjunasagar Dam across the Krishna River, 126 meters high and made of cemented blocks of stone. This dam was built using a highly labor-intensive technique, with innumerable workers clambering like ants up and down an enormous network of scaffolding.

Following the partition in 1947, India and Pakistan were involved in protracted and tortuous negotiations concerning riparian rights along the Indus, which is important for the irrigation of the dry northwestern areas of India. At times, the conflict of interests between the two countries reached such a pitch that they were on the brink of open war. The dispute was not resolved until 1960, with the signing of the Indus Water Treaty, which was drafted with the assistance of specialists from the World Bank. The treaty gave Pakistan the use of the three western tributaries of the Indus, and India control of the three eastern ones. Impressive irrigation works had to be constructed on the Pakistan side to compensate for the supply from the three tributaries ceded to India.

India has abundant hydropower resources, with an estimated economical potential of 41,000 MW. Only 7,500 MW had been harnessed by 1974, but developments are progressing quickly. New dams are often built to provide water for irrigation, as well as electricity generation, but three quarters of the country's electricity still comes from thermal power stations. The innumerable irrigation pumps are prodigal consumers of India's electricity output.

The scourge of floods

Although shortage of water creates great difficulties for agriculture during the dry season, the water surplus occurring in the rainy season also gives rise to a serious problem. Every year large areas of India, especially in the river valleys of the Ganges and Brahmaputra, are afflicted with inundations. At high water the Brahmaputra rises 4.5 meters in Upper Assam, where it is wide and shallow, and more than 10 meters in Lower Assam, where the river bed is narrow. Altogether, 20 Mha are threatened with flooding every year. To some extent, these floods are put to practical use for the cultivation of rice in the valleys, the rice being planted before the land is inundated. Naturally enough, flood control comes high on the list of Indian development priorities. During the past twenty-five years, heavy investments have been made in flood control projects. These projects normally involve integrated works including drainage and other measures to prevent waterlogging, as well as efficiently organized flood-warning systems. So far, 30 percent of the threatened acreage has been protected. Regular flood forecasts are organized on a substantial scale so that warnings can be broadcast in time for evacuation and relief measures to be organized in threatened areas.

Advanced water resource planning

Drinking water supplies began to be developed on a systematic basis during the 1950s, and India has made considerable progress in this respect compared with many other developing countries. About 75 percent of the urban population have access—albeit inadequate—to main water, and about 50 percent are served by main sewerage facilities. There are programs for the continuing extension of water supplies. Determined efforts are being made in the full awareness that India's future depends on the development of her water resources. It is estimated that about 920 km^3/yr, or

98

55 percent of the country's total water resources, can be exploited, just over two-thirds of this amount from surface water and about one-third from groundwater.

The population of India is expected to reach 900 million by the year 2000. This population will need an annual water supply of 970 m³ per capita, which represents a 70 percent increase over the present-day per capita requirement of 560 m³. Consideration has begun to be given to the possibility of artificially raising the country's precipitation rate. If, for example, an additional 10 percent of the moisture could be extracted from the powerful airstream of the southwest monsoon, the country's total rainfall would rise by 50 percent, which in turn would lead to a substantial increase of river discharge. The following plan of expansion has been drawn up for the period ending in the year 2000:

Purpose	Annual water requirement, km³	
	1971	2000
Irrigation		
surface water	246,7	666
groundwater	98,6	148
Water supply		
public	12,3	32
industrial	3,7	55,5
Power production	8,6	111
Total	369,9	1 012,5
Total water supply	1 678	1 678
Potential water supply	920	920
Percentage of total	22 %	60 %
Percentage of potential supply	40 %	110 %

India's per capita water resources are not very large: they are in the region of 3,000 m³ per annum. The situation is not helped by the uneven distribution of these resources in time and space. There is a surplus in the north and a deficit in the west and south. This has led to the idea of a National Water Grid as a possible means of correcting the maldistribution of natural resources. The intention is for the grid to link the natural rivers together by a system of canals, most of them running from north to south (see map, p. 101). Fully developed, the National Water Grid will comprise the following links:

1. the Ganges-Cauvery link, between the Ganges in the north and the Cauvery in the south;
2. the Brahmaputra-Ganges link;
3. a canal from Narmada to West Rajastan;
4. a canal from Chambal to central Rajastan;
5. a canal from Mahanadi to the coastal areas in the east (Orissa and Andra Pradesh); and
6. links from the rivers west of the Western Ghats to the drier eastern side.

The grid will draw on both river water and groundwater, and the water flow in certain stretches will be reversible according to the season of the year. The water resources of the Ganges, the main source supplying the entire system, are quite sufficient. During the first stage, 1,150 m³/sec will be diverted during the four months when the river is in flood (over 28,000 m³/sec). In this way the system will be fed with 12.5 km³ water. The water will be lifted to a high reservoir with an effective capacity of 25 km³, enclosed by a 460-meter-high dam. From here, the water from the Ganges will be distributed to the irrigation channels. The capacity of the distribution network will not be fully used except during drought years, when the strain on water supplies is greatest. According to current plans, the average level of utilization for a longer period of years will not exceed 40 percent.

The National Water Grid is a highly advanced project in that it will facilitate the coordinated utilization of surface and groundwater along lines similar to those applied in Israel, where the National Water Carrier System is fed with water from the Jordan and conveyed all the way down to the Negev desert. The system involves the reuse of waste water, which is to be purified and then discharged into the sand, through which it will percolate to form groundwater. The volume of water stored in the groundwater reservoir is to be kept under continuous computerized surveillance. India is also planning to use surface water to replenish depleted supplies of groundwater. For this reason, the total storage space to be provided includes groundwater reservoirs. In this respect, however, India's plans are at present more

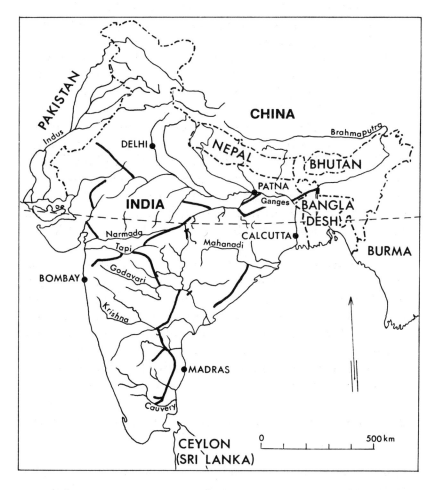

The drainage network in India and Bangladesh. The thick lines represent canals and tunnels planned as part of the National Water Grid, which will transfer irrigation water from the Ganges and Brahmaputra to areas with water deficits.

qualitative than quantitative, since reliable basic data about the size of groundwater reservoirs are to a great extent lacking. However, the Ganges Plain has considerable potentialities for the storage of groundwater. Storage on a significant scale is also expected in Gujarat, in the sandstone beneath Rajastan, in the Tapi valley, and in the water-bearing strata of the Krishna and Godavari.

Realization of the sophisticated plans that have been drawn up will require new legislation and greatly improved coordination at administrative level. A central water supply authority will have to be established for the entire country. At present the management of water resources comes within the jurisdiction of the individual states, and, so far, the national authorities have been able to do little to prevent time-consuming conflicts between states concerning water rights. Needless to say, this greatly impedes the progress of plans for irrigation and power production. Advanced plans for the designation of water as a natural resource belonging to the entire nation have been drawn up. In this way water will be brought under federal jurisdiction, which is one of the vital prerequisites for the establishment of the National Water Grid.

India today is said to be pervaded by a new optimism and by a slow transformation of the more indolent attitudes which formerly prevailed. Politicians and engineers are said to have acquired new strength, and the grandiose plans for a National Water Grid bear incontrovertible witness to a new sense of purpose. The implementation of these plans, however, will demand an immense effort in which the experience of more advanced countries may be extremely useful.

Bangladesh—the country which is inundated by its neighbors

One of the most urgent and pressing problems in Bangladesh is to produce enough food for its undernourished and rapidly growing population. Every year the cultivable acreage of the country is exposed to drought as well as to floods and periodic cyclones. The pressure of population is already enormous. The country's economy is founded on agriculture, which involves most of the 90 percent of the population living in the countryside. Grain is the principal ingredient of popular diet, and 95 percent of it takes the form

102

of rice. The rice crop per hectare, however, is very low.

The development potential of this poor and densely populated country is very much dependent on the possibilities of integrated control of water supplies. Bangladesh occupies a very special position, because it lies mainly on the combined estuaries of two of the world's largest rivers, the Ganges in the west and the Brahmaputra in the east. More than half the country is less than 7 meters above sea level. The land is extremely fertile, composed as it is of the rich estuarine silt which the two rivers have deposited. On account of the monsoon climate, Bangladesh suffers from tremendous water surpluses during the violent monsoon rains, when the rivers bring excess water not only from Bangladesh itself but also from vast areas of India, the neighboring country. During the rest of the year it suffers from devastating droughts when the river flow is at its lowest. Ninety-three percent of the area drained by the two rivers lies outside Bangladesh. The peak flow at the common outlet of the two rivers, which form a single delta in the Bay of Bengal, is 5,000,000 m^3/sec. Owing to these enormous flows of water, 40 percent of the cultivated acreage of Bangladesh is inundated every year. To this must be added the effects of flooding of coastal areas, where 12 percent of the cultivated acreage is exposed to inundation from the sea as a result of high tides or because of tidal waves generated, for example, by tropical cyclones.

The climate of Bangladesh, like that of India, is tropical and amenable to all-the-year-round farming, but the short monsoon season allows only one harvest. The rest of the year is too dry and the land has to be left fallow. Even the monsoon is unreliable at times, and rainfall may be deficient during critical periods. Now that practically all cultivable land has been brought under the plough, Bangladesh's only hope of feeding its starving population lies in irrigation, partly to insure the harvest of the monsoon season against the risk of a monsoon failure, and partly to facilitate two or even three crops per year.

Organized irrigation was not started in Bangladesh until about 1960. Irrigation can draw on surface water from the rivers as well as groundwater, which is available in large areas of the country either in a shallow aquifer about ten meters below the ground surface or else in a highly productive aquifer lying at a depth of about 100 meters. The monsoon rains appear to save the country from problems of soil salinization; the violent summer rains flush out the salt which has accumulated in the soil during irrigation in the preceding dry period.

Intensive planning is now in progress to bring the water resources of Bangladesh under control. The principal aim of water development projects is to improve crop yields. This demands a combination of irrigation, drainage, and measures to protect the country against the disasters of inundation. At the same time, safeguards must be provided for the great volume of waterborne transport, rivers being the vital nerves of the country's communications system. Fishing will also have to be protected as the second most important occupation in Bangladesh. Water-resource projects will also have to provide facilities for hydropower production and for the protection of coastal areas from penetration by saltwater from the sea.

The low flow of the rivers is insufficient to meet the country's water-supply and irrigation requirements. A serious threat is now seen in the plans now being developed by India for the diversion of water from the Ganges. A scheme of this kind would make it possible for practically all dry season water in the Ganges to be transferred to the Cauvery in southern India. Although, as we saw in the preceding section, India is planning to divert the copious excess flood only during the high-water flow season, the reaction from Bangladesh is understandable, more so when one realizes that Bangladesh has absolutely no possibility of storing the excess water supplies of the monsoon season in large reservoirs of its own because the country is predominantly low-lying. This also results in Bangladesh having a very limited hydroelectrical potential: all that exists today is a small hydropower station generating 80 MW. The lack of facilities for storing the flood water is obviously a serious disadvantage. It means that Bangladesh is entirely dependent on its powerful neighbor India for adequate flood protection. It is worth noting that the Ganges diversion project is already planned to reduce the high-water flood in the river.

For protection against inundation, which is one of the most urgent requirements, Bangladesh is now having to build protective banks along the river, and a 230 km containing bank was completed along the western shore of the Brahmaputra in 1968. This method of containing the flood water is not as effective as one might be led to suppose. The banks are usually designed with previous high-water marks in mind, but the enclosure of the water between narrow banks raises the water level as there is no possibility of altering the volume of water. The water is prevented from running out over the plain, which previously helped to keep the water level down. Consequently, one has to be prepared for higher floodwater levels when a river is embanked in this way. We shall return to consideration of this problem in the section on China.

Thus Bangladesh is almost entirely dependent for its future prosperity on its powerful neighbor and upon international cooperation in controlling the two international rivers which constitute its principal source of water supply. An equalization of the uneven flow of the Ganges and Brahmaputra can only be accomplished outside the frontiers of Bangladesh. At the same time, a diversion of water from the Ganges to the south of India during the dry season would be a serious disadvantage to Bangladesh, which depends on the dry season flow of the river for essential irrigation. A joint Indian and Bengali River Commission has been set up and has recently embarked on work which will be of immense importance to both countries.

China—skilled since ancient times in taming the waters

The People's Republic of China ranks with India and Central Europe as one of the most densely populated areas of the world. Its area is almost 10 million km² and it has a population of more than 700 million, which means that one

out of every four members of the human race is Chinese. The
average density of population is 70 p/km², but because most
of the population lives in the eastern half of the country, the
population density there is more than twice this figure.

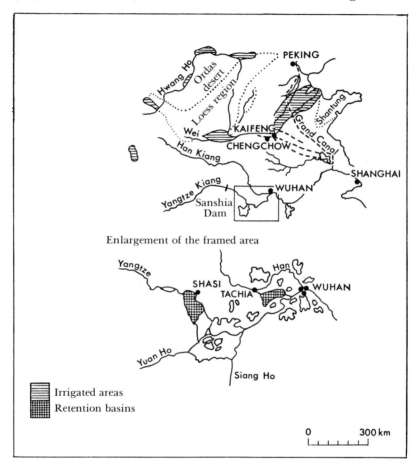

*Map showing the lower river basins of the Yellow River (Hwang Ho) and Yangtze-
kiang. The lower portion of the map is an expanded version of the frame-area in the
upper half and shows the retention basins in the Yangtze-kiang. The broken lines
in the upper half of the map indicate canals.*

China has a mean annual precipitation of 630 mm,
ranging from over 1,600 mm in the coastal areas and islands
of the southeast to less than 200 mm in the relatively dry

northwestern region. The distribution of precipitation fluctuates considerably both in time and space. China's water problems are dominated by the flooding of fast rivers and their heavy transport of mud. Irrigation is an obvious necessity in large areas, and in some places it has been practiced time out of mind.

Central China, east of the Great Wall and the highlands of Tibet, mainly comprises three large river basins, namely (from north to south) the Yellow River (Hwang Ho), the Blue River (Yangtze-kiang) and the Si-kiang (see map, page 106). These three great rivers play a vital part in the life and development of China. The Yellow River carries water from the high plateau of Tibet across the relatively rainless plains of northern China. The Yangtze-kiang comes from the same region and flows eastward across central China. The Si-kiang, in the south, which rises on the eastern slope of the high plateau, is far smaller.

The civilization which has emerged in China through the millennia has resulted from a fruitful interaction of man and nature, between the watered higher parts and the flooded lower parts of the great plains of the Yellow River and the Yangtze-kiang. Retaining control of water has been a consistent theme of Chinese history, in which prominent parts have always been played by the hydrologist and the civil engineer. The close dependence of Chinese civilization on man's ability to control water in the natural environment has been directly bound up with exceptional features of the country's physical geography.

Both the past and the future of China focus to a great extent on the two great river basins, namely those of the Yellow River and the Yangtze-kiang. Both rivers pass through the Yellow Plain on their way to the sea, and they are interconnected by several canals. Central China is usually divided into northern, or classical, China and southern China. The former comprises the Yellow Plain, the Heights of Shantung, and the Shansi-Shensi plateau, which is made up of very fine-grained loess. The Yellow Plain is dominated by rain-fed agriculture; not more than 10 percent of this area has ever been irrigated. Wheat is the main crop. The Great

Wall of China follows the western boundary of the loess region and coincides more or less with the 400 mm annual precipitation boundary, which is regarded as the boundary of traditional farming and therefore, in a manner of speaking, the natural line of demarcation between territory of the Chinese peasants and that of the nomadic population, which lives on the grazing of livestock. The Si-kiang area, in the south, is constantly fed with delta material carried by three rivers from the crumbling mountains. The depositional area has a population density of more than 1,000 p/km². The area is watered and drained by an intricate network of canals which are constantly having to be dredged to keep them from being silted up by the mud, which at the same time is a very important fertilizer.

The untiring struggle against the Yellow River

The Yellow River crosses the Yellow Plain 5-10 meters above ground level, between naturally formed embankments. For this reason it does not drain the Yellow Plain. The river has a high-water flow of 24,000 m³/sec and a low-water flow of about 240 m³/sec. It carries a great deal of mud, partial deposition of which raises its bed by an average of no less than 3 mm annually. Thus, the river bed has risen 1 meter in 300 years. During the past 3,000 years China has suffered 1,500 inundations and 26 changes in the courses of rivers, 9 of them extremely violent.

When the river bursts its embankments, which happens several times every decade, the streams and lesser rivers draining the cultivated plain are choked with mud. Seen in a long-term perspective, the deposition of mud replenishes the fertility of the soil and consolidates the plain. The immediate effect of this type of breakthrough, however, takes the form of devastating inundations. From time immemorial people have built barriers to enclose the course of the river, hoping that the water will flow into the sea as quickly as possible. As we have already seen in the section on Bangladesh, however, one direct consequence of these barriers is to

108

narrow the river bed and cause more frequent inundations.

As the Chinese empire grew, transport routes became more and more important to its rulers. Just before the beginning of the Christian era, a canal was built along the Wei valley at the lower end of the great bend in the river. The route of the canal was northwards to the capital, which at that time was deeper inside the valley, and the canal water was also used for irrigation purposes.

At Kaifeng, a little to the east of the same bend in the river, the Yellow River enters the Yellow Plain proper. From this debouchment the river has changed its course on several occasions, sometimes to the north and at other times to the south. Downstream of this point the course of the river is fairly steep, falling two meters in every kilometer. Three attempts have been made to lead off water in canals running southeast, but they have been only partially successful; the canal has been a lively artery but has then silted up within a very short time. The most important of these canals was cut during the 7th century A.D. and was the forebear of the Grand Canal built during the 14th century for the shipment of rice to the new capital founded by the Mongols at Peking in northern China. This canal cut cleanly across the natural drainage system—an enterprise which cannot have been undertaken with impunity in an area whose rivers carry such large quantities of mud.

During the first half of the 19th century the Yellow River was neglected, and almost too much care was taken to keep the canal clear at its vulnerable intersection with that river. In fact, efforts to protect this passage and to enclose the river to prevent inundations were so successful that the Yellow River was forced to seek an outlet further upstream. This change in the course of the river proceeded by stages during the floods of 1835, 1841, and 1843. By the time the 1855 flood receded, the entire reach of the river had swung northwards and the river now intersected the Grand Canal at another point, with the result that the canal ceased to be navigable.

Several times during the centuries, the embankments of the Yellow River have been opened for defensive reasons. In 1642 the declining Ming dynasty opened the flood defenses at

Kaifeng in a fruitless bid to halt the southward advance of the Manchurians through the country. This action was repeated in 1938 when Chiang Kai-Shek opened the defenses at Chengchow in an equally fruitless attempt to halt the advance of the Japanese invaders. This time the floods cost the lives of 900,000 peasants, and large areas of land were rendered useless for about ten years.

The water problems of present-day China are the same as previous generations have had to contend with. A constant struggle is waged both for and against water. Drought and soil erosion are the farmers' greatest problems in the loess region. The Government of the People's Republic of China has shown great energy and ability in dealing with water problems. Not only must the Yellow Plain be protected from inundations, the water must be used constructively, particularly as drought, not floods, has been the true cause of many agricultural disasters in this area of low precipitation, where farming suffers from a chronic water shortage. The entire project is of mammoth dimensions and will ultimately comprise forty-six dams at various points along the river generating a total of 23,000 MW of electrical power. Most of these dams will have to be built in the loess region, where the river collects most of its mud. Owing to the high mud content of the river water, the reservoirs behind existing dams silt up rapidly. Efforts are being made to gain a respite by planting trees and building terraces to prevent the rainwater from carrying so much mud into the river. Active, disciplined, and extremely methodical efforts will be required from the entire population if the new dams in this highly sensitive area are to be kept functional. The battle against drought in the Yellow Plain has also been joined, and a great deal of the water of the Yellow River is now being used for irrigation. Hundreds of thousands of modern pumps are in operation, and irrigation is expected to double the agricultural output of the Yellow Plain. Matters are greatly complicated, however, by the salinization resulting from irrigation, although this is far from being a new problem.

The gigantic projects on the Yangtze-kiang

In contrast to the Yellow River, the basin of the Yangtze-kiang is an area where droughts are rare. Rice is the staple crop. In terms of river discharge, the Yangtze-kiang is the third largest river in the world. Every year it carries 2,000 km³ to the sea; as we have just seen, this is more than the entire water resources of India. The discharge area of the Yangtze-kiang is inhabited by 250 million people. Like the Yellow River, it cuts its way through the mountains in a deep gorge, which then opens out into a plain where the mud carried by the river is discharged to form fertile soil.

Large shallow lakes in the lower reaches of the river act as surge basins for the annual high-water flow, which can be very high indeed. A large number of tributaries flow into this area, and one of them alone—the Han River—discharges twice as much water as the Yellow River. Despite the constant and steadily rising threat of inundation from the river, this is the largest rice-producing region in China. The country's largest center of heavy industry is also located here. But the position at the junction of the Han and the Yangtze-kiang is extremely vulnerable. The control of the Yangtze-kiang, required to afford sufficient protection against the risk of flooding, is a vast undertaking. A 200-meter-high dam 4 km long is now being planned for the Sanshia gorge. The project includes a power station which will generate 20,000 MW. The dam will be the second largest in the world. However, China is not yet economically prepared for this project, and in the meantime the tributaries have been dammed, and two artificial retention basins have been enclosed to hold the flood water. One of them, Shasi, is 900 km² in area, and the other, Tachiatai, is slightly smaller. The construction of the Shasi basin was a remarkable achievement, said to have been built in 75 days by 300,000 workers without the aid of advanced machinery.

River and canal traffic has always been important in China and will remain so. In view of the difference of climate, which makes the crops of the two great river valleys mutually complementary, north-south communications are at least as important to China as communications between east and west. The Grand Canal has now been restored and is navigable for vessels of up to 3,000 tons as far as Peking. There are also plans for additions to the canal system to link Peking in the north with Canton in the south.

Before the establishment of the Communist regime in 1949, hydrological observations were of relatively poor quality. Consequently, reliable data are only to be had for the past twenty-five years, which is far too short a period on which to base a reliable assessment of flooding risks. A technique has had to be developed whereby use can also be made of high-water data from a long time ago. Local inhabitants are interviewed, and high-water marks carved in rock faces, etc., are studied to ascertain the level of floods which occurred many years ago. The figures on page 114 show the difference between an assessment of the risk of high floods based on data from the past twenty years and a corresponding assessment based on data including the great floods of 1794 and 1853. Work on the development of this technique began after the flood calculated about 1950 as being liable to occur once every thousand years had been greatly exceeded by the floods of 1956 and 1963. A frequency graph taking both historical floods into account had given far more reliable indications; according to this estimate, the high water liable to occur once every thousand years is 30,800 m³/sec, not 8,400 m³/sec as estimated previously.

Finally, it is worth noting that the extensive constructions now being planned do not really imply any innovation. On the contrary, they represent the consummation of the work and dreams of thousands of years. Bearing in mind the extraordinary capacity displayed by the Chinese for working by simple means, the task they have now taken upon themselves may well be within the bounds of possibility. Between 1949 and 1960, and largely by dint of manual labor, they are said to have shifted quantities of soil comparable to the building of two Panama Canals!

112

Asia's way to the future

Documents from the Rome conference give the following outline of the future prospects of Asia. Demand for food is expected to rise more rapidly in the Near East than in any other developing region. Here as in other areas one encounters the two most common obstacles to development: lack of qualified people capable of communicating technical insight to the rural population, and the unwillingness of farmers—either for economic reasons or lack of motivation—to adopt new practices. But another obstacle to development, and one which is more prominent here than in any other part of the world, is shortage of water. As can be seen from the water shortage map on page 3, large areas of the Near East are as seriously short of water as the Sahara. The water available in the Near East is the water of the great rivers, groundwater from the mountain areas, and a certain amount of ancient deep seated groundwater. Water has always been a limiting factor in this part of the world. In unirrigated areas, the rural population, whose numbers are rapidly rising, is entirely at the mercy of the sporadic rains, with the result that harvests fail completely every ten years or so.

The most immediate requirement in these areas is to achieve better management of the water resources which have already been harnessed through the existing irrigation arrangements. Leakage losses must be reduced, drainage must be improved and the incipient salinization must be stopped. Salinization is now having a prejudicial effect on a large proportion of the irrigated acreage, and at times it can reduce harvests by half. The problem is particularly acute in the areas surrounding the Tigris and Euphrates. The new-found wealth of the oil-exporting countries of the Middle East have provided ample resources for investments in agriculture. The bottleneck in these countries is now lack of experienced personnel.

In the Far East, otherwise known as Monsoon Asia, are the most important rice-growing areas in the world. This region

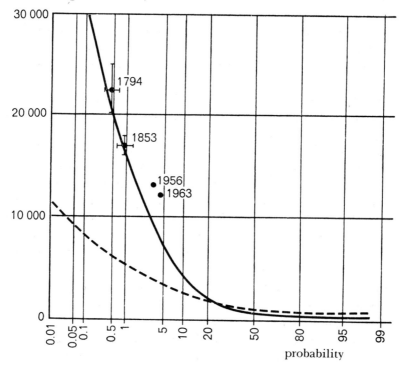

Annual high water flow, m³/sec

Frequency graphs for different maximum floods in the Hutuo River. The lower line is based on twenty years' observations up to and including 1954. The upper line is based on the same figures together with reconstructions of the floods of 1794 and 1853. The chart also shows the high floods of 1956 and 1963, which greatly exceeded the forecast based on the lower graph line.

holds 70 percent of the population of the developing countries, and as we have already seen, many of these countries are very densely populated indeed. Relatively speaking, however, the expected growth rate in population for the period ending in 1985 is moderate—2.6 percent for market economy countries and a mere 1.6 percent for planned economy countries. In absolute figures, however, this indicates quite considerable population increases for the coming ten years; food will have to be found for about 60 million more people. What then are the prospects for agricultural development in this region?

114

As we have observed several times, practically all cultivable land has already been brought under the plough. In India this is more than half the total area of the country. In this part of the world, therefore, the strategy for technological development will have to focus on improving productivity, i.e., the yield from the acreage which is already being cropped. Yields can be raised by increasing the number of harvests and by increasing the yield in each harvest. In both cases the development of irrigation is absolutely vital, the most urgent requirement being the renovation, modernization, and expansion of existing irrigation works. Many such facilities will have to be combined with proper drainage for agriculture to be viable. In the longer run, new irrigation works will have to be provided. Although this region already contains more than 60 percent of the irrigated acreage of the third world, irrigation could be more than doubled. Plans to this end, which have been presented by the FAO, provide for the extension of irrigation to 15 Mh during the period ending in 1985. Attention is being drawn to the three possible means whereby these facilities can be supplied with water: large-scale irrigation works can be supplied with surface water, minor facilities can be occupied with low-level pumps (cf. the Nile Valley, p. 83) and use can be made of groundwater on a greater or lesser scale. As we saw in chapter 3, small-scale developments will probably be of the greatest short-term importance, by virtue of their greater flexibility and smaller planning requirements. Groundwater is of great interest as a source of water supply in view of its ready availability in large areas of the Far East, but we have to bear in mind that the unrestrained use of groundwater is liable to result in overexploitation and falling water tables.

6 South America—a generously watered continent

On the whole, South America has abundant supplies of water, but it also provides an excellent example of the uneven way in which water is distributed. If, for example, we compare the runoff from the continents of the world, about 25 percent of the grand total comes from South America. On the other hand, South America contains less than 15 percent of the world's total land area. By way of comparison, Africa accounts for about 10 percent of total runoff, and its land area is about 23 percent of the grand total. Some of the largest rivers in the world flow through South America. The rivers of Brazil alone discharge at their estuaries about one-sixth of the world total of fresh water flowing into the oceans.

Although South America as a continent has plenty of water, it includes a number of regions with severe water problems. Even the well-watered areas have difficulty in surmounting problems connected with the organization of their water resources, due to the rapid growth of their populations. More and more water is needed for the various activities of mankind. The following table shows the increase in population forecast for Latin America:

year	population in millions
1970	283
2000	652
2025	1 072
2050	1 409
2075	1 575
2100	1 608
2125	1 610
2150	1 689

These figures, taken from one of the preparatory documents compiled for the UN World Population Conference in Bucharest in 1974, represent the forecast termed "medium variant." As can be seen, the population of Latin America is expected to quintuple within the next 100 years. Other works presented to the same conference show that its urban population, which in 1970 was about 56 percent of the total, is expected to rise to about 76 percent by the year 2000.

Brazil—a dominant country as regards water resources

In attempting to characterize the water situation in South America, one is bound to devote a great deal of attention to Brazil. To start with, Brazil is one of the largest countries in the world in terms of area. It encompasses 8.5 million square kilometers and it has a population of over 100 million. It is drained by some of the largest rivers in the world, the greatest being the Amazon. The Parama is another of the country's major rivers.

Some idea of the capacity of the Amazon may be gained from the fact that it discharges into the Atlantic a volume of water ten times that of the Mississippi in North America. Observations at Obidos, about 650 km from the Amazon estuary, have shown that the river at that point discharges 6,300 km^3 annually.

The runoff area of the Amazon is incredibly large, amounting to some 6,200,000 km^2. It is bounded to the north by the high plateau areas of Venezuela and Guyana, to the west by the Andes and to the south by the Brazilian mountain range and the Mato Grosso bush region. The Brazilian mountain range also constitutes a water shed between the Amazon basin and the runoff area of the Paraguay-Parana system, which comprises about 3,160,000 km^2 (see the map on page 118). The two last-mentioned rivers enter the sea in the La Plata region, in which Buenos Aires is situated. Most precipitation in the Amazon basin falls as rain; snow falls only in certain highland areas. It is, therefore, important to examine variations in precipitation. Studies of this kind are

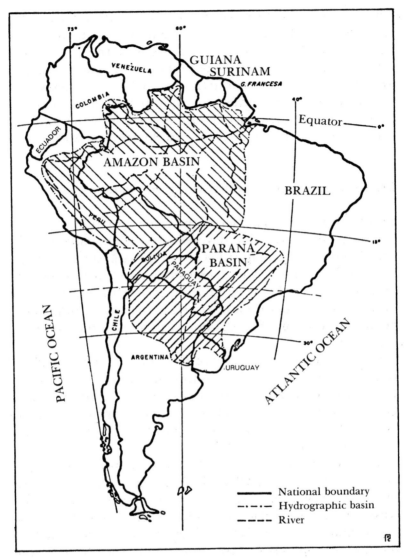

The Amazon and Parana basins.

made not only in Brazil but also in Peru and Ecuador, i.e., in the eastern part of the Andes, where the Amazon rises. Mean annual precipitation in the Amazon's runoff area is about 1,500-2,500 mm. In that portion of the runoff area of the Parana which belongs to Brazil, precipitation is between

118

1,000 and 2,500 mm. These are very high figures by global standards. The global mean is probably about 800 mm.

Even in Brazil there are areas where precipitation is by no means high. One example is the highland area along the eastern coast of Brazil near Recife. Recife itself receives a mean annual precipitation of 1,500-2,500 mm from the trade winds, but the 1,000-meter-high mountain ranges relatively near the coast are an effective barrier to the transport of moisture further inland. On account of this shelter effect, the interior of the country has an annual average rainfall of no more than about 400 mm.

The water problems which are likely to arise in connection with the expected 3 percent annual growth of population call for extensive planning. Water management is greatly handicapped by being divided between many authorities. It is feared that difficulties may be encountered in establishing a concerted, uniform management of water policy. Today questions concerning water supplies are handled by six ministries out of Brazil's total of twenty-four administrative units. The main focus of interest is two principal activities in the water sector, the development of hydroelectric power and the organization of water supplies for urban areas and industrial activities. As we have seen, the urban population of South America is expected to grow rapidly toward the close of this century. Unfortunately, it does not appear to be easy today to achieve a unifying and firm management of water supply. Despite this, there is a great deal of activity. There are many projects in progress including, for example, a large number of dam construction schemes which will facilitate a better control of water supplies by provision of new reservoirs. PLANASA (Plano Nacional de Saneamiento) is a particularly active organization which aims to provide water of acceptable quality for 80 percent of the urban population by 1980. This is regarded as an average achievement figure, because the goal has already been achieved in certain parts of Brazil. The project is a large one and is expected to cost about $136 million, to which must be added the cost of developing an irrigation network covering about 450,000 hectares.

The tropical rain forests of Brazil

As was mentioned in the chapter on Africa, parts of the area adjacent to the Equator—10° north and south of it—are covered by tropical rain forest. The Amazon region of Brazil forms part of this tropical rain forest. The forest is a peculiar and complex ecological system, characterized by certain relations between its essential components—production, consumption, and degradation. A typical feature of the rain forest system is that practically all the nutrients are stored in the trees and plants themselves—very little is stored in the ground. As soon as parts of plants die and begin to decay, a process of nutrient absorption begins in the surviving plants.

The tropical rain forest exhibits many "defensive attitudes." The immediate absorption of nutrients is seen as a form of defense against the leaching process whereby the heavy precipitation would otherwise wash the nutrients away. The absorption process is highly efficient, as witness the low concentration of mineral ions in the Amazon and other rivers which drain the tropical rain forest. In the Manaus region—on the Amazon—the leaves and other detritus falling to the ground in the tropical rain forest have been found to contain about 18 kg calcium per hectare. But the quantities present in the river itself are so small as to defy measurement. It is also relevant to note that precipitation contains relatively large quantities of nutrients. In the Manaus region, one year's rain was found to bring with it about three kg phosphorus, two kg iron, and ten kg nitrogen per hectare.

One defensive position is based on the fact that seeds and fruit are the staple food of living animals in the tropical rain forest. Some protection is afforded against the depredations of these consumers by certain tropical trees and plants whose seeds contain poisonous substances or have an exceedingly bitter taste which repels browsing animals. It is typical of the tropical rain forest that it comprises many species but few individuals of each kind. A species which bulks very large is generally found to have developed a characteristic defense

120

mechanism of the kind described here.

Even the tropical rain forest of Brazil—where many people believe our civilization started and where others see the "granaries" of the future—has been subjected to rapid and widespread destruction. Trees are felled and the soil is burned. But as we have just seen, if trees and other vegetation disappear, the plant nourishment disappears with them, so that before long the land becomes uncultivable, and new areas have to be cleared to replace it. The abandoned soil is no longer protected by vegetation from the fierce rays of the sun, and alternating periods of rainfall and drought prepare the way for erosion and complete destruction of the soil. There is a great deal of this destructive activity in the Amazon region. In fact, the region today provides only half the food required by the two million people who live in it. In economic terms, it contributes only 1 percent of the Gross National Product (GNP) and at the same time has to be given 3 percent of GNP to keep it alive.

Another cause for grave concern is that there is no immediate hope of curbing the devastating slash-and-burn technique which is practised in the rain forest. Obviously a more intelligent and ecologically conceived policy will have to be implemented if the rain forest is to survive. People must realize that the secondary forest which grows up does not have any of the properties possessed by the first, primary forest. The secondary forest grows faster, it is weaker and it does not live as long as the primary forest. Its average life is perhaps 20 years, compared with several hundred for the original forest. The short-lived secondary forest is succeeded by one of a different quality, which grows more slowly than the secondary forest and survives longer. Estimates indicate that it takes hundreds of years for a new rain forest to evolve.

The Paraguay River and its inundated areas

The Paraguay River, which rises in the Mato Grosso region, is one of the great rivers of South America. On its way to the sea it flows through the great Pantanal zone, a waterlogged river plain of about 50,000 km². This zone lies in a catchment area of about 400,000 km² bordering on the Amazon and Paraguay rivers. It is fairly flat and is, on average, between 50 and 140 meters above sea level. The zone floods easily, and when this happens, the floodwater moves slowly down towards Asunción in Paraguay and Rio de la Plata. This inundation area covers between one and three Mha. The Pantanal zone is sparsely populated. Most of its inhabitants are engaged in cattle raising.

Strangely enough, very little is known about these flooding effects. Very few technical and scientific studies have been made, for instance, of the mechanics of inundation in these parts, and very few field observations have been made. One reason for the lack of data is the poor communications existing between the areas which are liable to flood. In order for better use to be made of the zone, a close study will have to be made of its hydrological conditions, particularly as the overbank flooding affects traffic on the Paraguay River as well as the cattle farming.

In January 1956, the UN Development Programme (UNDP) sanctioned a Brazilian proposal calling for a comprehensive hydrological study of the upper Paraguay River. The main preoccupation was to chart the area hydrologically to be able to forecast inundations. Improved hydrological knowledge would also make it possible to take precautions along the river and its tributaries. The main target of the project became the establishment of a hydro-meteorological system in the upper catchment area of the river and the making of observations to provide documentation for hydrological studies within the Pantanal zone. A study was also to be made of certain environmental effects. The results of these supplementary studies would make it possible to assess the need for a high-water early-warning system. This system included no less than 115 stations. The findings, published in 1973, showed that the mean annual precipitation for the three-year period studied was between 1,400-1,700 mm for high areas and 900-1,000 mm in the low-lying areas of the Pantanal zone. This is below the mean values known previously from these areas.

It was also established that precipitation fluctuated a great deal from day to day in the low-lying areas. There was less daily variation in the highland areas, and precipitation was more persistent than in the northern mountain areas. It was also interesting to note that the rainy period came between September and April and that it was brief in the northern parts. During the "dry" period, rainfall was far more frequent in the southern than in the northern part. This revealed that the watercourses of the northern region—unlike those in the southeast—varied in a way which was more typical of a tropical climate. Scientists have opined that the low precipitation figures referred to above may reflect a climatic change in the catchment area of the Paraguay River.

The hydrological and meteorological project also included topographical studies. The most characteristic feature of the Pantanal zone is its flatness. The east-west gradient was found to be roughly 0.3 to 0.5 m/km, while the north-south gradient was far less—1.5 to 3.0 cm/km. For this reason, the Paraguay River flows very slowly, with the result that when the river is in flood, large areas are inundated. Some of this water infiltrates, and some continues to flow above ground level. A portion of the surface flow is restored to the river further downstream, and some of it is trapped in cut-off meander bends, known as oxbow lakes. The hydrological studies showed that the water supplied to these oxbow lakes was not returned to the river. There is reason to supposed that the floodwater thus trapped later infiltrates to augment the groundwater reservoir.

The hydrological studies also served to establish that a great deal of water "disappeared" in the Pantanal zone. This was ascertained by means of water balance studies in which a check was made of the amount of water entering the zone and the amount leaving it. In the course of a three-year period it was found that 960 m^3/sec were brought into the area and 810 m^3/sec carried out of it. In other words, an estimated 5,000 million m³ "disappeared," i.e., 5 km³ per annum after allowance was made for evaporation losses. This dry three-year study led to the conclusion that no reliable indication could be given of the mean flow of the Paraguay River and that no reliable estimate could be made of the losses in the Pantanal zone during wet years. Inundations seemed only to occur when two consecutive wet years followed a long succession of dry ones.

A mathematical model of reality, of the kind previously used in the Columbia region of the United States and in the Mekong area in Southeast Asia, was constructed for forecasting purposes. The flow coming into the northern part of Pantanal is available. The aim with the help of the model is to describe storage in the Pantanal zone and then to describe the flow at various points further downstream. The model has been based on the measurements taken, and also on air photographs and topographical studies of the zone. With the aid of this model, it is hoped to arrive at a description of what happens in the zone both at high and low water.

This UNDP project is of great importance not only to Brazil but to the whole of Latin America. It is essential for the project to be continued by means of observations and analyses, in order to make possible the forecasts which are so important to the country itself and to the rest of the continent. These forecasts, short-term or long-term, are the essential foundation of a wise development policy for the region as a whole. The prime concern must be to establish facilities for a more efficient assessment and organization of opportunities for farming, cattle raising, and navigation. But this is not all. Guidelines must be drawn up for a water-supply policy in this region.

Peru's water deficit

The areas of South America which we have been considering so far are areas which normally have a good supply of water. Peru, on the other hand, is chronically short of water. The climate of the country varies a great deal, both temporally

124

and spatially. Moreover, the topography is such that certain regions are very hard to penetrate. The coastal region consists in part of desert-like plains crossed by rivers whose flow is highly irregular. Attempts, therefore, have to be made to regulate water supplies by the construction of dams and reservoirs. Because precipitation is insufficient—sometimes the mean value is not more than 100 mm per annum—a coastal irrigation network will have to be developed. It is impossible now for new land to be broken in the mountain areas, but irrigation can be used to improve the yield of land already under cultivation. The forest areas are of poor fertility, and great efforts will be needed to improve their quality.

Floods rise in the mountain areas, which are extremely wild and impassable. The flow is uneven, and water is only available for a short period—three or four months—in the year. The rest of the year is characterized by an extreme drought. This poses problems to farmers, because it is hard to predict when water will be available. These hydrological factors are a serious impediment to agricultural development, particularly in the coastal region, which, as we have just seen, hardly receives any rainfall. It is important, therefore, to economize in water use, and there are very strict laws and regulations laying down practices and priorities for water supply, not only in the coastal region but also in the mountain region. Farming in the mountain region is a very "dry" activity, owing to the lack of rainfall. Here again, complicated civil engineering projects of a special kind are needed to solve the problems of water supply. The laws and regulations applied to the mountain region are different from those applied to the coastal region.

Water is a limiting factor which also impinges heavily on other sectors of society. The power industry, mining, and public services all need water and this necessitates further measures designed to guarantee the fulfillment of their quantitative and qualitative requirements. Mining, which plays an important part in the development of Peru, demands large quantities of water, which gives rise to serious problems of supply. River pollution is a serious problem in

Peru, because effluent from industry and human settlement is discharged into the rivers on which industrial facilities and communities are situated. Long periods of drought, combined with the problem of pollution, have prompted the enactment of extensive legislation concerning ownership and priorities in the matter of water supply at both national and sectional levels.

South America—a continent with plenty of water and plenty of problems

As we have seen, South America has an abundance of water, with the exception of certain parts of the continent, such as Peru, and yet it has serious water problems. Documentation (in the form of sufficiently comprehensive observations) is generally lacking for water supply forecasts. At the same time, the population of South America is growing rapidly, and swift action is needed to establish a proper management of water supplies. But this does not exhaust the list of difficulties. Together the Amazon and Congo basins (the latter in Africa) make up an area of almost 400 Mha of potentially cultivable land. The climate of these regions is such that precipitation is more than adequate, and there are very few, if any, dry periods. There is an equally large potentially cultivable area in the peripheral regions surrounding these river basins, but this area is affected by droughts which can last up to six months.

In short, there are about 800 Mha of land which are only partially utilized at present, although they are well supplied with water. Unfortunately, the soil is often so lacking in nourishment—especially in South America—that we do not know how it can be improved sufficiently to raise its productivity to an acceptable level. A great deal of research will be required to find the solution to this problem. Perhaps there are certain transferable conclusions to be drawn from conditions in Florida; fifty years ago we were at a loss for methods of fertilizing the sandy soil there.

The allocation of cultivable land in South America also

presents great problems, because there is plenty of perfectly good but sparsely populated land, while, on the other hand, the most densely populated areas are those with poor soil. Thus, extensive problems remain to be solved in South America. Good land is not always to be found where there are large numbers of people, and water resources are not easily managed.

7 *Problems ahead for the industrialized countries*

Mean values can be misleading

In chapter 2 we considered the global water situation, and we made various estimates of needs and resources in different parts of the world. In that connection we also noted the great problems that are already having to be faced in Asia, and we saw that a serious aggravation of the situation can be expected towards the end of the present century. While on the subject of water supplies in the developing countries, we also referred to the emergent problems of water supply in Africa. But it also transpired from our account that the water problems of the future would not be confined to the developing countries. Problems could also be expected to arise in the industrialized countries, and we mentioned that Europe would be particularly vulnerable in this respect.

In this chapter we shall examine some of the problems of the industrialized countries more closely, and we shall also study examples showing that the mean continental values on which we based our pronouncements may sometimes be misleading. This is because the water needs of different countries can deviate to a greater or lesser extent from the average value for the continent of which a country forms a part. There are countries whose needs are higher than the average value, and it is with reference to these countries that the graphs of water demand—expressed as percentages of runoff—shown in chapter 2 may have given a more optimistic representation of conditions than is justified by reality.

What do Balcerski's values for Europe have to tell us?

Let us begin with conditions in Europe. Earlier we said that, for practical purposes, the stable part of water supply was a better yardstick of water resources than the total available quantity. But we also mentioned the Polish scientist Balcerski, who set out to investigate the actual difficulties which would arise gradually as consumption in each country approached the level of the stable part of its water supply. We also mentioned that his fundamental aim was to relate these water problems to the economic problems of each country. It will also be recalled from Balcerski's analysis that if water demand exceeded 20 percent of the total amount of water available, we could be certain that the handling of water questions would have a major bearing on the total economy of the country concerned. If, on the other hand, demand proved to be less than 5 percent of the total amount available, the question of water supply could generally be solved without any serious complications. Meticulous studies were carried out for all the European countries, and the findings can be summarized as follows:

Countries using less than 5 percent of the total quantity of water available	Albania, Austria, Finland, Iceland, Ireland, Norway, Sweden, and Yugoslavia
Countries using between 5 and 10 percent	Belgium, Denmark, Italy, Rumania, Spain, Switzerland, Turkey (European), the UK, and the USSR (European)
Countries using between 10 and 20 percent	Czechoslovakia, France, Greece, Luxemburg, the Netherlands, Poland, Portugal, and West Germany
Countries using over 20 percent	Bulgaria, Cyprus, East Germany, Hungary, and Malta

The map of Europe on page 131 shows national values for percentage utilization of total runoff according to Balcerski. In considering these figures, one should bear in mind that the stable part of European water supply is 45 percent of the total. As can be seen from the map, the heaviest pressure on water supplies is in the northern part of Central Europe and in the fringe states of the eastern bloc. It should also be said, however, that the significance of the information yielded by these Balcerski values must not be exaggerated. These figures are mean values reflecting the average situation of a given country, so they cannot convey the individual variations occurring within the country. It is impossible to characterize the water situation of an entire country in a single figure.

What else does the map of Europe on page 131 have to tell us about the water problems of different countries? Compared with the map at the front of the book, it tells us that extremely difficult water problems occur in countries combining high industrial potential with a low level of real water resources. Hungary, Bulgaria, and East Germany, for example, have serious water problems, and the water resources of these industrialized countries—measured in terms of specific runoff—are the smallest in Europe, amounting to something between 2 and 4 liters per second per km². This makes between 65 and 130 mm per annum. By way of comparison, the average for Sweden is 11.7 l/sec per km², making 270 mm per annum. In the countries utilizing between 10 and 20 percent of their total water resources, runoff is probably between 120 and 260 mm per annum.

International rivers

Water problems are also liable to arise in countries sharing the use of water from an important river. In view of the heavy utilization of water resources which characterizes these countries, a great deal of work needs to be devoted to the solution of their mutual problems of water supply.

Efforts have been made to define principles for matters of this kind by drafting international rules of law. At present, however, these rules can only be classed as recommendations. The most important proposals are those which were presented at an international legal conference held in Helsinki in 1966. In those recommendations it is said that regulation of the common use of water must be founded on a

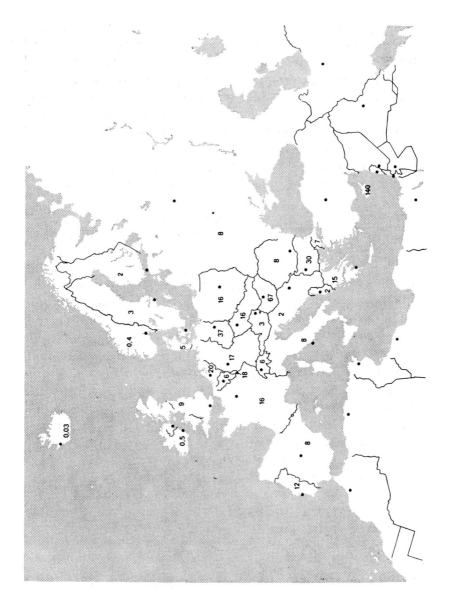

The figures denote Balcerski's values for the various European countries, i.e., the proportion of total water resources (the runoff derived from precipitation) utilized for water supply.

mutual understanding of economic and social water requirements within the various states utilizing a common river.

Proposals have also been put forward concerning the factors which should be taken into account with a view to establishing a fair apportionment of common use. Particular care is to be devoted to the handling of pollution questions. A fundamental principle here is that effluent discharged into a river by one riparian state must not be liable to cause demonstrable inconvenience to a user of water from the same river in another country.

Complications of this kind are illustrated in the recommendations by two states—A and B—collaborating on an irrigation project in which they both use water from a reservoir situated in state A. Both states, then, derive benefit from this reservoir in their irrigation activities. It has now transpired that the irrigation enterprise is gradually raising the salt content of a watercourse flowing through a third state C. The reservoir, moreover, has been constructed in this watercourse. The rising salinity will have an increasingly detrimental effect on the irrigation of areas in C. Legally speaking, therefore, states A and B are under a clear obligation to take steps to prevent their joint water management from having substantially harmful effects on state C.

In many cases, it is difficult, in the event of a dispute, to establish the burden of guilt stemming from the common use of water. Special difficulties are involved in the computation of the economic liability which may be incurred by one of the implicated states. We have already witnessed a number of international "accidents" of this kind, one of the most recent of them being the fish death in the Dutch part of the Rhine, which was attributed to the discharge of effluent in the West German part of the river.

Water problems of some of the European countries

In chapter 2 we saw that the predictions made for Europe as a whole indicated that water demand, compared with present day figures, would rise by almost 50 percent by the year 2000, i.e., in less than 25 years' time. This is a predicted average increase. If the prediction is applied to individual countries whose water resources are already heavily exploited, the figures for these countries will be very much higher. In Hungary, for instance, an increase on this scale would mean virtually 100 percent utilization, while in Bulgaria and East Germany it would mean 45 and 60 percent respectively. All three figures are higher than the stable portion of water flow. How then are we to deal with these problems?

One way is to try to store surplus water; another is to transfer water from surplus to deficit areas. But there are other possibilities. For instance, water can be recycled for industrial use and private consumption reduced by means of a revised tariff policy. As far as industry is concerned, however, a very high level of recycling indeed will be required to bring about substantial savings.

Let us now turn to a closer consideration of the water situation in two European countries. We have chosen the Federal Republic of Germany and the Netherlands for this purpose.

The problems of the Federal Republic of Germany are rapidly increasing

The total available quantity of water in the Federal Republic of Germany is probably in the region of 100 km³ per annum. Most of the surface-water supply comes from the Rhine. The available part of surface and groundwater resources can be estimated at 46 km³ per annum. The total present-day requirement for public, industrial, and agricultural use is about 16 km³ per annum. These figures show that the Balcerski value in the map on page 131 is a relatively good indication of water use in the Federal Republic. Cooling-water demand is not included, and this can be estimated at 14 km³ per annum. By the year 2000 these figures are expected to have risen to about 28 and 44 km³ per annum respectively, the latter figure including cooling-water demand.

A future water demand of 28 km³ per annum gives a Balcerski value of 28, which is almost twice the present figure, not far from the stable portion of European water resources, which is 43 percent. Groundwater extraction for the year 2000 has been estimated at 16 km³ per annum, which means that practically all groundwater will have to be utilized, as well as surface water extraction at double the present rate.

The Federal Republic has a large number of conurbations with heavy concentrations of industry. These include the Ruhr, the Frankfurt-Wiesbaden-Mainz-Darmstadt complex, Brunswick and Hanover, to mention but a few. In all these areas, natural-water resources have been inadequate, and exceptional measures have had to be taken to solve the problems of water supply.

The Ruhr is presently supplied from a number of reservoirs on adjoining higher ground. The purpose of these reservoirs is to guarantee that the Rhine maintains a flow of 20 m³/second through the Ruhr. Most of the extracted water is used for domestic supply. The extra water thus added to the Rhine is thought to reduce the risk of pollution. Industrial effluent presents a more difficult problem, but a chain of purification plants has been set up along a tributary of the Rhine into which the effluent is channeled.

Some other areas employ a different type of water supply system. Bremen, for instance, has difficulty in maintaining domestic supplies of water. The River Weser should be able to supply Bremen with all the water it needs, but this river is heavily polluted. Moreover, it suffers from additions of saltwater. Water is, therefore, transferred to Bremen through pipelines from remote areas of the country—the Harz mountains, which are 250 km away. The water problems of Stuttgart are partly solved in a similar manner. Transfers of this kind are expensive and for industrial purposes the cost would be prohibitive. Other methods are, therefore, being tried. One such method is to divert water from nearby rivers by canals. It is possible in this way to raise the low-water flow and with it the water quality of rivers within the reach of industry.

The Germans are fully aware of the problems of water supply they have to contend with, but they are confident that the total quantity available will still be sufficient in the year

2000. The main difficulties are thought to lie in the purification sector and in introducing to industry new processes which are less prodigal of water. As we have just seen, the total demand for water in the year 2000, excluding the demand for cooling water, is expected to reach 28 km³ per annum—practically equal to all the surface water available. Even if every available drop of groundwater is extracted, there will be a further need for 14 km³ of surface water per annum.

Whatever method is adopted for the management of surface and groundwater resources, the flow of polluted water is bound to be disturbingly large. Great efforts are, therefore, needed to solve the problems of water pollution. The fact is that these problems are already enormous. The Federal Republic is seriously concerned over the pollution of groundwater. Needless to say, surface and groundwater resources are not mutually isolated. Groundwater is also polluted to a certain extent by fertilizers used on the land and by seepage from refuse tips, etc.

Despite all these difficulties there is optimism concerning the future of water supply and confidence in the possibilities of solving the problems. Some of the greatest of these problems occur in the northern part of the country, where they are partly being solved by means of transfers. The question of transfers from Sweden, which was raised some time ago, may have to be reconsidered at some future date.

In the Netherlands groundwater has to be kept free from ocean salt

The second European country to be considered is the Netherlands. Water supply in this country is derived from both surface and underground sources. The largest sources of surface water are the Rhine, draining from West Germany, and the Neuse, flowing from France. One of the characteristic features of the situation in the Netherlands is the problem of saltwater intrusion from the sea, which damages both surface and groundwater sources. The Delta Plan is a bid to solve this problem by various technical means, including a shortening of the coast line. Many of the problems of saltwater intrusion are connected with the system of locks required for inland waterways. Owing to the different densities of saltwater and freshwater, the former intrudes every time a lock is opened. Efforts are being made to counteract this phenomenon, e.g., by means of specially designed locks.

Another saltwater intrusion problem is bound up with the fact that 75 percent of the area of the Netherlands is below sea level. Urban expansion almost invariably leads to a lowering of the water table, which makes it easier for saltwater from the sea to penetrate. Domestic water supply in the Netherlands consists of about 65 percent groundwater and 35 percent surface water.

The composition of industrial water supply is reversed— 20 percent groundwater and 80 percent surface water. The problem is, however, that reserves of groundwater will have been exhausted by about 1980 if domestic water supply continues to contain about 60 percent groundwater.

Reservoir storage is already being practised in places where the salt content of the surface water is acceptable. The reservoirs are filled as completely as possible when water of good quality is available. Present-day water problems are solved in this way. The water of the Rhine, however, presents serious problems. It can only be stored after its salt content has been reduced. The Netherlands appear to be facing serious problems of water supply, and the feasibility of seawater desalinization is being investigated.

Californian water supplies are quite inadequate

California has long been engaged in large-scale water supply projects. The northern part of the state has plenty of water, derived from the rains coming in from the Pacific. The southern part, on the other hand, is mostly desert. The two parts are separated by the deep Central Valley, which is entered by two rivers, the Sacramento and the San Joaquin;

see map on page 138. These two rivers enter the sea through the delta near San Francisco. A great deal of water from the San Joaquin is used for irrigation, but the flow is insufficient for effective use in the southern part of California, which has about 10 million inhabitants. The supply which can be administered to this part of the state, about 1.2 km³, falls short of total water requirements there.

A large number of aqueducts and dams have been built over the years to solve these problems. One of the biggest aqueducts was built as long ago as 1913. Most of the transfer water comes from the north of California, whence it has to be carried for a distance of some 700 km. Today, three major aqueducts carry water to southern California—namely, the Los Angeles Aqueduct, the Colorado River Aqueduct, and the California Aqueduct. When the last-mentioned of these becomes fully operative, it is expected that 4.5 km³ will be supplied to the southern area each year.

Water has been transferred from Colorado since the beginning of the twentieth century

Some appreciation of the problems involved in building these aqueducts will be gained from the following data concerning the Colorado River Aqueduct. This aqueduct flows from the Colorado River to a reservoir (Lake Matthews), but on the way it has to cross a desert and several mountains. Altogether, it comprises about 500 km of canals, conduits, tunnels, and five pumping stations. The pumping stations lift the water between 45 and 155 meters, and altogether, the water climbs 500 meters. This aqueduct was originally planned to carry 45 m³/sec, but recent droughts in the south of California necessitated supply of 54 m³/sec. This has been achieved by enlarging the pumping stations and keeping the canals filled. Today the water leaves the final pumping station by three routes. Two of these serve direct runoff, while the third leads to the Lake Matthews reservoir, where water is stored until needed. This reservoir normally has an active storage capacity of 145 million m³.

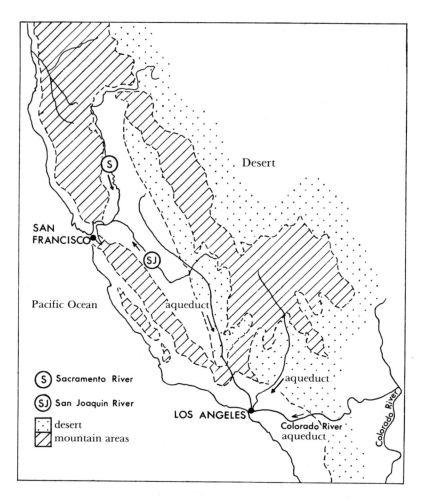

Reservoir storage and transfers of water have had to be resorted to in order to meet California's water requirements.

The transfer of water from the Colorado River has sufficed for domestic and public needs during the past thirty years, with enough water left over for agricultural purposes and replenishment of groundwater reserves. The last of these functions is by no means unimportant, because it helps to save the groundwater reserves of the entire region from exhaustion. Some surface water is also used to replenish the groundwater in zones near the coast, as part of a scheme to prevent saltwater intrusion from the Pacific.

Salinity has become more and more of a problem with the passing of the years. In 1972, the U.S. authorities prescribed a maximum salt content of 500 mg/l. Measurements taken during the years the Colorado River Aqueduct has been in use show that the salt content has risen steadily. By 1968, the long-term mean level was 740 mg/l. If nothing is done about this problem, the salt content is likely to rise to 800 mg/l by 1980 and 1,110 mg/l by the year 2000. In 1973, proposals were put forward for the removal of 400,000 tons of salt from the river every year. It was estimated that this would cost $125 million but more realistic estimates indicate a cost of more than $455 million.

Today southern California also gets water from the north

By 1950, it was realized that the water obtainable through the Colorado River Aqueduct would be outstripped by the expansion potential of southern California. Attention was then turned to northern California, where there is plenty of water, so much in fact that inundations are common when the rivers overflow. The transfer of water throughout the entire length of the state was obviously a task for the state authorities. About $1.6 billion were allocated for the construction of dams, reservoirs, etc. As mentioned earlier, the water will be transported over a distance of 700 km. On the way, it has to be lifted a total of 1,100 meters with the aid of pumping stations. This project is unlikely to be completed before the turn of the century.

Water from northern California is of far better quality—in terms of salt content—than the water of the Colorado River. This generated the idea that the water of the Colorado River Aqueduct should be improved by mixing it with water from the north. This has been permitted only at points where salt concentrations can be kept under meticulous surveillance. It is believed that, by combining suitable proportions of water from the various conduits, a mixed water can be obtained with a salt content varying between 375 and 500 mg/l.

It has been decided to charge a higher price for the superior water coming from the north. The extra cost of the better quality water was about $4 per m³ between 1971 and 1973 and about $8 per m³ between 1973 and 1975. Now that the different qualities are being mixed, a careful note is kept of the proportions to insure that the user pays the correct price for the water he receives.

The gigantic NAWAPA plan

An even more grandiose plan was presented recently under the title of the North American Water and Power Alliance (NAWAPA), which as the name implies is a combined water-supply and power project. The basic idea is to harness water which would otherwise run into the sea. The essence of the plan is illustrated by the map on page 141. Areas of water shortage in Canada, the United States and northern Mexico are to be supplied with water from rivers in Alaska by means of this transfer system. The realization of these plans will involve the construction of a large number of dams, power stations, tunnels, and canals. The output capacity of the power stations is forecast at 110,000,000 KW. The project is estimated to take between twenty and thirty years to complete. The water to be supplied under the plan was originally estimated at about 130,000 million m³, i.e., 130 km³ per annum, but it is assumed that the project can be enlarged to provide about 300,000 million m³. The preinvestments for this project are expected to total about $114 billion.

The United States has other water problems as well. Between 1962 and 1966, the northeastern part of the United States suffered a very severe drought. To take one example, the supply to New York City was on the verge of failing in the summer of 1965. The city is crossed by the Hudson River, but this water could not be used because it was so heavily polluted by household waste and industrial effluent. The irony of the situation was that there was plenty of water on hand, but none of it could be used.

140

The NAWAPA project in North America involves the transfer of water from well-watered areas in the northwest to areas of water shortage in the south and east. The nucleus of the project is an 800-km-long artificial lake in the Rocky Mountains, between Montana (in the United States) and Canada. A gigantic, navigable canal takes the water down to the prairies, linking the artificial lake with the Great Lakes.

People in the United States are fully aware of the difficulties involved in maintaining water supplies in some areas. The United States is another example of an area which has an uneven temporal and spatial distribution of water resources. This is already apparent from the instances we

141

have quoted. It is also understandable that the description of the North American water situation given in chapter 2, where we presented average water-demand figures, should be subject to considerable local fluctuations. In the average terms of the account given in chapter 2, no serious problems of water supply are to be expected until almost the end of this century. In fact, we know that they have already arisen in many parts of the United States, and we know that they are serious and intractable. Some people would go as far as to say that in the United States the water crisis is graver than the fuel crisis.

What is the transfer cost for water?

The examples of water problems of industrialized countries given in this chapter have served to show that efforts are being made, both in Europe and in North America, to solve water shortages by storing water in reservoirs during high-flow periods. This water can then be drawn on during periods of shortage. Alternatively or in combination with this method, water can be transferred from other areas, near or far, where more abundant supplies are available. As can be seen from the description of the plans for NAWAPA, heavy expenditure is involved; in fact, it is so heavy that this particular project is not considered feasible in every respect. The Aswan Dam, to which we referred in an earlier chapter, is another example of a costly storage scheme. One naturally asks how the profitability of such mammoth projects has been calculated. In this section we shall consider, very briefly, some aspects of the economics of water transfer. Without going into detail on the subject of costs, we shall consider factors bearing on the viability of a transfer project.

If we stand beside a beautifully situated lake with clear water in which we bathe during the summer, and if we are asked how much it costs to provide the water to which we have such convenient access, our natural impulse is to say that it costs nothing. Water is all around us, in lakes and in rivers. As soon as any attempt has to be made to alter the quality or quantity or move the water, we discover that it does, in fact, cost something.

To improve the quality of the water at some point in a river, a treatment plant has to be built. To change the quantity, a canal is necessary in order to transfer the water from one river to another. If—as in the examples already given—a reservoir is necessary to increase supplies, then it will cost money to build a dam. To lift water from one level to another requires pumping and this has to be paid for. How do costs of this kind vary, and how are costs related to our conviction that more and more water must be made available for particular purposes?

The three examples in the figure below show the variation of costs in three types of situation. The first instance shows how costs are effected by an increase of river flow. To begin with, the river is used as it is—line a in the figure—and this costs nothing. Then a dam is built in order to create a reservoir. This involves a certain initial cost, b. The cost rises as the storage capacity is enlarged (line c). The next figure refers to the purchase of water from a neighboring country. Here again, heavy initial costs are involved, as is witnessed by the initial steepness of the graph lines. When the amount has to be increased beyond the capacity of the source, the expense may rise steeply if it becomes necessary to purchase and transfer water from increasingly remote sources. The

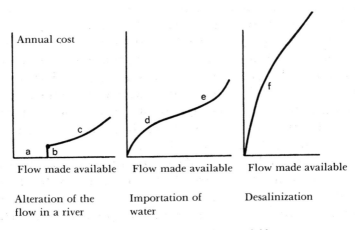

Alteration of the flow in a river

Importation of water

Desalinization

Three examples of the cost of making water available.

143

third figure illustrates the costs of desalinizing water and conveying it over a distance. Here again, heavy initial expenditure is involved. A desalinization plant has to attain a certain capacity before a maximum return is obtainable.

What is the value of water?

So far, we have been speaking of the value of water. When discussing such questions as water transfer, it is not enough to know the cost of water; one also has to know its value. Is there any difference between cost and value? Perhaps the simplest illustration of the difference between them is that drinking from a clear spring costs nothing, but it may nonetheless be of great value to the drinker. In the obverse, it may cost an enormous amount of money to pump water up to the top of a high mountain, but the effort may be quite valueless.

An attempt has been made to distinguish between cost and value by defining them as follows. The cost of water is what has to be paid in order to provide a specified amount at a given time at a particular place. The value of water may be defined as the largest sum we are prepared to pay in order to be supplied with that amount at the required time and place. This distinction between cost and value is of fundamental importance when planning the transfer of water.

Let us examine the practical importance of the distinction. Imagine a land area where water flows in a river running through an area which is virtually untouched by human use. The river then continues into the sea. Its water is not used for anything. If someone were to have the idea of increasing the flow in the river by artificial means, it might be said that the effort was pointless. But this does not mean that the water lacks intrinsic value. Suppose the water could be diverted from the river and sold to a neighboring country in need of additional water. The value of the water, then, would lie in the possibility of its being used for different purposes within that country, e.g., power generation, recreational purposes or an inland waterway. As long as the water is in its natural state, there exists a certain natural balance. But what happens if it is diverted to the neighboring country? If the balance of nature is altered, the ecological system may be disturbed with disastrous effects on fish, wildlife, etc.

Water as an export commodity

The value and cost of water are among topics requiring the negotiation between two or more states proposing to embark on a water-transfer project. Points of this kind can easily give rise to disputes. We end this cursory discussion by considering the way in which the terms "cost" and "value" are used in a practical context. The diagram below illustrates how the exporting country tries to evaluate its possibilities for selling water. The procedure adopted is to investigate the rise in costs which will be entailed by making increasingly more water available. The diagram shows three curves, for 1970, 1980, and 1990 respectively. The value of access to water can

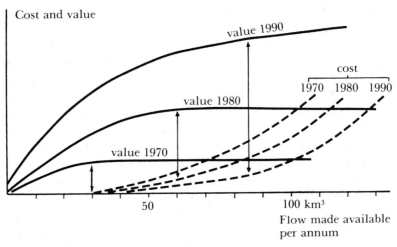

Cost and value of water in the exporting country.

be similarly calculated on the basis of the benefits to be derived by applying water to irrigation, power production, etc. It can easily be seen that demand for water is determined by the greatest vertical distance between the cost line and the value line. For 1970 this is 30 km^3, for 1980 this is 60 km^3, and for 1990 this is 85 km^3.

The reason why demand stops at these values is as follows. If, for example, we consider 1980 and follow the cost line to the right of the vertical arrow, we find that costs have risen far more rapidly than value. In other words, we obtain less value per cost input than at a water flow indicated by the vertical arrow. The purchasing country can also establish similar measurements for the relationship between value and cost. Seen from the latter country's point of view, it transpires that the need for water is rising, but that a rise in demand would involve a heavy increase in costs as compared to the rise in related value. The importing country can then see whether water can be purchased more cheaply from the exporting country. The exporting country, in turn, can then calculate the amount of water it can sell without the venture becoming uneconomical.

Concluding observations

We have tried in this chapter to outline some of the water problems of the industrialized countries. The problems of Federal Republic of Germany and North America are founded in the ancient hydrological truth that there is sufficient water—at least, sufficient for a long time to come—but that the supply is unevenly distributed in time and space. This gives rise to problems of storage and transfer when water has to be provided for household, industrial, and agricultural use. The costs of supplying water by such "artificial" means are several times higher. There are many western states in North America where irrigation projects receive such large measure of economic support that their intrinsic profitability becomes too low for irrigation to be justified. In Arizona, for example, 90 percent of water resources are applied to irrigation without an equivalent contribution being made towards state income.

As we saw earlier, a water crisis has existed in California for many years. At one time this was the sole problem, but now that more and more complex engineering methods have been introduced to transfer water in response to rising needs, fresh problems have arisen. At one time, it was possible to compute the profitability of a project by considering the expenditure on it and the income from it. Strict estimates of this kind are now being queried more and more as a result of growing environmental awareness. Conservationists complain that the full consequences of interventions in the natural scheme of things which these storage and transfer projects imply cannot be foreseen. Nor can an economic value be put on the damage caused to the ecosystem. So long as we are unable to quantify these aspects, we will be incapable of devising the most economical solution to a given problem of water planning. The simple fact is that we have no figures concerning ecological effect which can be put into the estimate. This creates a feeling of uncertainty, causing us to look for other solutions whose implications and consequences are within the scope of our prediction. We shall return to this point later. This chapter has been concerned with making the point that even the industrialized countries are already beset by serious problems of water supply. However, an optimistic view is taken of the prospects of finding safe solution to these problems in the future—a future that will present even greater demands on quality and quantity, if the current population trend continues.

8   *Water management is quite possible*

Recapitulation

The reader who has reached this chapter may be excused a sense of confusion about prospects for a solution to the world's water problems. We have shown that, even if consumption remains within the average figures for different continents, water requirements will in many areas be so high that to provide for them will be exceedingly difficult. This, we found, was particularly true of Asia, but in Africa and Europe, it has also been shown that considerable problems of water management will have arisen by the year 2000, i.e., less than twenty-five years from now.

Moreover, our account of conditions in North America showed that, even if the average figure for water requirements in that continent as a whole did not suggest any imminent serious water problems, a detailed analysis revealed that within individual states variations are so great that considerable difficulties surround both present and future solutions to local water problems. But even here—as in the special account given of the water supply problems of the Federal Republic of Germany—we found that there was optimism about finding solutions.

Clearly a great deal of trust is being placed in the combined ability of hydrologists, water resource engineers, and environmentalists to overcome the problems. There is, perhaps, a natural reason for buoyant optimism, water being one of the essential prerequisites of our existence. But what are the prospects, in purely general terms, of solving the problems concerning our water resources? In this chapter we will attempt to describe some of the means or methods whereby, in our belief, present and future problems of water management can be solved.

148

The IHD, 1965-74

It is perhaps appropriate to begin with the IHD organization. What is the IHD? The letters stand for the International Hydrological Decade, an international program sponsored by UNESCO. By the end of the program almost 110 states were actively involved in a ten-year plan aimed at analyzing the world's water resources. The IHD started in 1965 and ended in 1974. These worldwide activities were prompted by an awareness of the rapid growth of human water requirements and the need for wise and scientifically based planning of the utilization of water resources. The desire for an international organization of this kind did not emerge spontaneously; the guidelines for the IHD were drawn up after a debate in the UNESCO General Assembly in 1964. The IHD was a scientific program with several parts. These included an appraisal of the state of knowledge of hydrology and water resources of the world; standardization of instrument observations, etc.; establishment of networks for data collection; research on hydrological systems and on specific hydrological problems; training and education in hydrology; and systematic exchanges of information. Among the topics studied were:

1. water balances;
2. the composition of natural waters;
3. erosion, river bed development, transportation, and deposition of sediment; and
4. human influence on hydrological phenomena.

These various fields of hydrological activity are perhaps self-explanatory, except for the first one. The purpose of the water-balance studies was to investigate the various components of the hydrological cycle, such as precipitation, evaporation, runoff, and groundwater formation. This part of the program was vitally important for water supply.

Hydrology deals with questions concerning continental water, and a sound knowledge of a country's hydrology is

149

obviously important to its water supply. To solve this problem, an international study of the various items included in the hydrological cycle was organized. A number of representative catchment areas—i.e., areas surrounded by watersheds and representative, both climatologically and geographically, of an individual country—were selected and made the subject of hydrological field observations. Within these areas, some 3,000 in number, a continuous collection of data has been carried out. Data are needed for calculation purposes, but the difficulty, where hydrological problems and problems of water resources are concerned, is that measurements of this kind need to be taken for a considerable period of time—preferably thirty years in the general opinion—before any reliable conclusions can be drawn, e.g., about natural fluctuations.

The IHD has undoubtedly contributed towards the establishment of such observations. Universities, colleges, and national authorities have taken part in this collection of basic data. Activities of this kind have no constructive value unless the data are analyzed. This, in fact, is one of the dilemmas of research activities. It is relatively simple to collect large quantities of primary information; the difficulties arise when it comes to devising methods for the efficient and rapid analysis of the data. The analysis, moreover, has to be conducted in such a way that the findings can be used by those who are concerned with the practical handling of problems of water management.

In 1969, an appraisal was undertaken of the information obtained during the first half of the decade. It was found that the proposed ten years would be far too short a period within which to arrive at unambiguous results. In many countries the beginning of the IHD had been delayed for various reasons, but even in countries where a relatively early start had been made, the basic data concerning the quantity and quality of water which had been collected in the course of five years was not sufficient. Perhaps, one might say that the infancy of hydrology itself was part of the reason why ten years' work failed to yield all the facts and knowledge required for analysis of the water situation of today and tomorrow.

150

The IHP

The activities of the IHD were formally concluded at the end of 1974, but this was not the end of joint international activities in which about 1,500 active hydrological experts were involved all over the world. A few hundred of these experts took part in a conference in Paris at the end of 1975 to summarize the IHD activities of the previous ten years. It became clear during the conference that very impressive amounts of information had been produced by various countries in the form of published data, guide books, monographs, and scientific contributions on various important hydrological problems.

At the same time, it was established that the whole range of IHD activities had been enormously stimulating to the science of hydrology and, therefore, to the development of knowledge concerning the fundamental principles applicable to the management of water resources. One reason for the success of the IHD was undoubtedly the need for encouragement and support in the field of hydrology. At the beginning of the period, water-resource research was relatively limited, and there was relatively little coordination between the institutions and authorities active in this field.

The Paris conference made it quite clear that the hydrological effort must be continued and reinforced. There is still a tremendous shortage of fundamental data on the quantity and quality of water in different parts of the world. Representatives of the developing countries, among the delegates at this conference, were most insistent on the need for continuation of this work.

In 1972, the UNESCO General Assembly resolved in favor of the IHD being succeeded by long-term international cooperation under the title of the International Hydrological Programme (IHP). This program started on January 1975, at the termination of the IHD.

Like its predecessor, the IHP comprises a program of research and education. The main tasks of the program can be summarized as follows:

1. Provide a scientific framework for the general development of hydrological activities.

2. Pursue the study of the hydrological cycle and develop scientific methods for the determination of water resources throughout the world with a view to achieving a rational utilization of global water resources.
3. Evaluate human influence on the water cycle in relation to environmental effects generally.
4. Contribute towards a wider exchange of information on hydrological research and on new methods in hydrology.
5. Support education and training in hydrology.
6. Assist member countries in the organization and development of their national hydrological activities.

From this general program, three important project areas have emerged, which are considered to include the problems whose investigation genuinely demands international or regional cooperation. Another criterion governing these projects was that they must yield direct or at least potentially useful results. These results were to be of such a kind that they would genuinely improve the understanding of hydrological processes or could be used in predicting hydrological phenomena of demonstrable relevance to future human needs. The three major project areas which have now crystallized out can be described in terms of the following spheres of interest.

a. The natural water balance and its subsidiary processes; an estimate of water resources on various scales in drainage areas, states, regions, and continents and on a global level.
b. The effects of human activity on hydrological conditions in the broad sense, as regards the quantity and the quality of both surface and groundwater.
c. The application of new technology to the water sector, including remote sensing, the processing and analysis of data, forecasting, mathematical models, and system analysis.

The art of predicting the effect of man-made changes in nature

The IHP represents a clear shift of interest from that of the

IHD. Hydrology and water resource questions are central concepts in both research programs, but the more recent IHP activities put more emphasis on human influence upon the hydrological cycle and upon the effects that this produces. The IHD program, on the other hand, was essentially aimed at exploring the water balance and water resources in natural areas where human influence was not yet perceptible, or where human influence was so slight that its effects on hydrological conditions could be disregarded.

There is a definite train of thought behind the modes of procedure in the two hydrological research programs. The IHD was intended as a research and data collection program for the accumulation of information which would provide comparative material for a later study of areas affected by human activity. This kind of comparison with reference values was intrinsically valuable, but it also yielded a fund of knowledge that will facilitate a certain amount of prediction relating to the likely effects of subsequent plans for interventions in the hydrological cycle. In other words, a number of comparisons between areas affected by man and similar areas unaffected by man furnished information for the establishment of general principles applicable to other situations. We shall return to this idea shortly.

We referred to human influence on the hydrological cycle. There are many degrees and modes of influence. One of the primary forms of intervention is the removal of trees and other vegetation; clear-felling is the forester's term for this practice. This category of influence also includes extensive drainage, cultivation, and other methods of food production, digging wells, etc. The next stage of influence is excavating for buildings, asphalting of streets, diversion of water from watercourses, discharge of inadequately purified effluent into rivers, and so on. The third stage, that is, full urbanization, involves the development of an urban community with houses and streets as well as public, commercial, and industrial buildings. Rising population demands the establishment of new systems of water supply and water distribution. Use is made of artificial infiltration, new and deeper wells of higher capacity are drilled, and so on.

All of these stages, with the many different forms of interference which they involve, are directly matched by the influence exerted on the hydrological system. We will content ourselves with a single example. The asphalting of streets and roads, to which we have just referred, prevents the underlying ground from being infiltrated by precipitation. This means that the groundwater reservoir will not be replenished as easily and the water table may fall. Asphalting has other effects. Where precipitation is prevented from seeping into the ground, it will flow over the asphalted surface, and result in a concentration of the rainfall because surface runoff is much faster on a paved surface than on an unpaved one. This is the central idea behind what is now termed the stormwater problem. A great deal of research effort and money is now being devoted to seeking a solution to this problem of urban hydrology.

Models play an important part in modern research concerning water resources

In hydrology and in the water-resource sector, the increasingly complex picture presented by the total range of water activities has required a more general approach to problem areas. We need only consider the situation where, in a hydrologically limited area, we are faced with a number of activities all demanding water. There may be more than one urban community requiring water for domestic and general public needs, as well as industries, farming, and forestry, hydroelectric power stations, and others. There are likely to be a number of treatment plants, and the area may include more than one river, as well as lakes. As well as drawing on surface sources, the area may have groundwater resources which are used for supply. How is one to appraise this situation? Perhaps if the resources are limited, the question may arise as to how the available supply can be shared and what stipulations have to be made concerning the discharge of effluent into the watercourses in order to keep pollution below a predetermined level.

There are probably several answers to this question—several solutions, one might say. If further restrictions—and they may be necessary—are added to the problem, and if one decides to answer the question subject to the reservation that the cost of the "total process" must be as low as possible, there will probably be only one or a very small number of solutions. Solutions of this kind are produced by using mathematical methods to devise what is called an optimum solution. Even if mathematics is a useful aid to finding the solution of current problems, the procedure may involve considerable difficulties. These difficulties are related to our inability to put a price on all the constituent parts of our system.

In an earlier chapter, the difficulties of evaluating interference with our external environment were discussed. What happens when we interfere with various kinds of recreation environments? If we suddenly use this environment for other purposes, how can the changes be taken into account in our debit and credit system? What price are we to put on the environment? Environment interference of this kind gives rise to factors which are hard to evaluate. They are hard to evaluate because they cannot be compared economically with other forms of interference. But since we are forced to solve our problems of water resources, and since we prefer to solve them without excessively intuitive or random thinking, these factors, hard as they may be to assess, must be included.

One way to do this is to start by making an estimate without taking these noncomparable entities into account. After an optimum solution has been found without them, an attempt is made to discuss how these more intractable entities will influence the result which has already been obtained. Probably a range of choices still remains, because the environmental controlled, noncomparable quantities imply a certain flexibility, which makes it possible to arrive at an optimum acceptable solution.

There are other methods of solving such a complex system. One way is for evaluable and less evaluable factors to be taken into account from the beginning. One then has to develop a method which proceeds according to the best solution for the simultaneous fulfillment of two or more aims. One dual aim, for instance, is to keep real costs as low as possible in a project involving a series of activities demanding water, and at the same time to keep environmental interference to a minimum. This is an extremely difficult problem. With a certain amount of exaggeration, this can be described as the limit of the solutions of which we are capable at present. The solution of such problems demands extremely complex mathematical analysis as well as very high capacity computers.

The module is the area inside the water divide

What we have described is usually included under the concept of systems analysis, although this concept covers such a wide range that it does not always reveal the method or methods adopted for solution of the problem. It is reasonable to say that as we try to depict reality in schematic images, we construct models of reality. Perhaps some classification of the ideas which have just been put forward is now called for. The entire systematic procedure which we attempted to describe above can be broken down into smaller units. For example, one possible module in this breakdown is the catchment area, i.e., the area separated from its neighbors by a water divide. All water descending on this area in the form of precipitation leaves it either through evaporation or as runoff in the river which drains the area. An example of this kind of module is shown on page 157.

This runoff module is constructed in such a way that the natural state of the area is represented in the large circles symbolizing the presence of water in surface water, groundwater and soil moisture. Soil moisture is present in the layer of soil between the surface of the ground and the zone of aeration, i.e., the layer of the ground which contains air and is not completely saturated with water. The area is supplied with water as a result of precipitation (P) and, in certain cases, by in-flowing surface water (the arrow at top

156

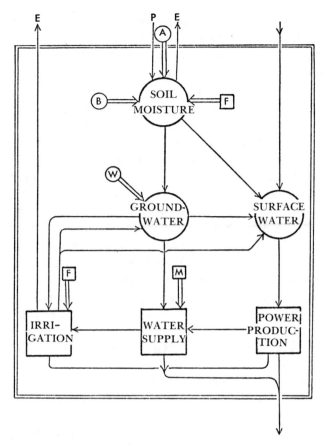

P   Precipitation
E   Evaporation
(A) Airborne salts
(B) Biological processes
(W) Weathering processes
[F] Fertilizers
[M] Municipal and industrial waste

Schematic description of a generalized runoff module (water resource unit) taking into consideration the balance of water and of substances dissolved in same. Large circles denote natural reservoirs; squares denote man-made reservoirs. Small circles denote natural sources of dissolved substances; small squares denote man-made sources of dissolved substances.

right). Water leaves the area through evaporation (E) and runoff (the arrow at bottom right).

When we exploit this area, we introduce the new reservoirs (marked by the squares in the diagram), and we store water for irrigation, water supply, and power production. This runoff module not only symbolizes quantitative use, it can also be used to reflect qualitative processes. Thus, the diagram shows the supply of dissolved substances through biological influence from airborne salts and the influence of erosion which is already going on in the soil and beneath it (small circles). To these forms of natural supply are added contributions which man makes to the water flowing through the area; e.g., fertilizers, as well as domestic and industrial wastes (small squares). Human waste affects the water in an area of this kind and disrupts its equilibrium. It may take a long or a short time for this to happen depending on whether the water reservoirs are large or small. We may expect it to take a long time when groundwater is affected, e.g., between 10 and 100 years for the effects of human activity to become apparent. Changes usually appear much more rapidly in surface water.

Now, perhaps we begin to understand why these studies of fundamental hydrological processes are so important to our ability to manage water resources correctly and plan their utilization in relation to quantitative and qualitative re- quirements. The runoff module can also be used to build up a more complex system (see the diagram on page 159) which is more practical when we have to describe a more complex pattern of water use.

We have now seen an example of the way in which hydrology is making increasing use of model versions of a true hydrological process. Models for the water balance and materials in a runoff area can safely be described as an indispensable tool for future water management and conser- vation. A large number of these water-balance modules will be needed to cover the most important runoff areas. Once the mechanism of these modules—i.e., water balance in terms of quantity and quality—has been properly mastered, they will provide an excellent aid for the control and prediction of the

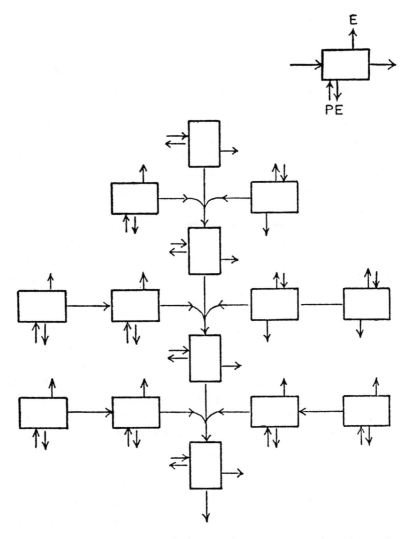

A model to illustrate the way by which a complete river area is composed of a series of water resource units for different subareas.

effects of changing forms of human interference on the water balance. In other words, knowledge concerning the function of the runoff model can be sufficiently improved to facilitate predictions of what will happen if more water is extracted from some point, or if the quality of the water is altered somewhere in the system. It is, therefore, the task of hydrological research to provide these tools of management, and a great deal of basic research will be required to this end.

The model generalizes and simplifies a complex reality

Before we leave this section on the use of models in hydrology, there are a few other questions which merit attention connected with the construction of models. The above discussion should have made it clear that the construction of models is a complex undertaking. The purpose of the model is to depict the natural environment together with the forms of human interference to which it has been subjected. At the same time, the model has to be as simple as possible without unduly distorting reality. Unimportant details which would merely complicate the interpretation of the water balance model should be ignored.

In order for the reader to understand the difficulties involved in working with models, one of the additional complications is introduced. This arises from consideration of the term "stable part of runoff," a term used several times in this book. The stable part of runoff can be equated with the low-water flow in a river—the minimum that can be guaranteed all the year round. A greater volume of water will flow in the river during one or more seasons of the year, and when this volume is at its greatest, it is referred to as high-water flow. Thus, river flow can vary within certain limits influenced by a series of external factors. It is hard to predict how the river will change with the passage of time. What allowance can be made for this in the model? What flow should be taken as the basis of calculations?

It is customary to distinguish between two ways of surmounting this complication. One way is to study the system for only a short period of time, in which case a particular flow can be established and used in the runoff model. The flow thus established is taken to represent the flow in the watercourse, and any minor variations are ignored. In other cases, there is reason to believe that the change of flow describes a pattern in time. This is a determinist approach.

Predictions based on this type of model have to be limited to short periods of time and the model used for short-term forecasts.

If, on the other hand, slow processes are to be depicted instead of fast ones, we have to find a way of relating them to the variation in time of the true flow. Runoff varies from year to year. As we saw earlier, this variation is particularly marked in the case of dry areas. Runoff may be very slight during certain years, and several such dry years may occur in succession. During years of abundant rainfall, the flow in the river may be very heavy. Flow variations of this kind are usually described with the aid of statistical relationships, and models of this kind are termed stochastic—a term applied to random processes occurring over a period of time. This type of approach to a hydrological problem normally involves far greater mathematical complications than the determinist approach.

An example of work in the stochastic sector of hydrology is provided by the questions which arise in the planning of hydraulic engineering and water-control projects. A study, then, has to be made of the effects which these enterprises would have had in normal wet and dry years. A study of this kind is usually based on an existing "historical" series of observations. Often, however, the series is too short and does not present a sufficient number of situations. Certain stochastic devices are then used to develop a number of long-term processes whose probability equals that of the "historically" observed processes. In simple terms, the collection of available examples is expanded to the extent required.

Engineering—a Swedish tradition

So far, we have been concerned with the work which has been done in the field of hydrological science in order to analyze basic hydrological facts which are mainly connected with the hydrological cycle, with or without human influence. We have already noted that the depiction of true hydrological processes in models is one of the many tools of hydrology. But hydrology is not only a theoretical science. Fundamentally, it is more of an experimental discipline. One of its basic tasks is to analyze and describe the incidence of water and its distribution between the continents—to study the physical and chemical properties of water and its interaction with the environment. There are many recipients of basic hydrological knowledge, recipients who adopt the findings of hydrology as a basis of calculation and convert them into practical knowledge in the field of hydraulic engineering. The water-resource engineer belongs to this category of recipients.

Swedish engineering has a long tradition of water management. This tradition was established mainly by work in the power sector. Highly sophisticated solutions of technical problems in the treatment sector have also been found and in the context of water supply, Swedish engineers have made particular progress in solving problems of groundwater management. During the past decade, rapid developments in the fields of hydrology and water-resource management, and also in the environmental sector, have placed additional demands on our technical knowledge relating to management of water resources.

The cooperation required between different types of expertise is illustrated in the diagram on page 163. The leading "dramatis personae" in this joint management of water resources are the water-resource engineer, the hydrologist, and the environmentalist. As can be seen from the diagram, each expert has his own part to play in the common endeavor. It is interesting to note the relationship between the hydrologist and the environmentalist. There is good reason to expect that in the future the environmentalist will be able to pay less and less attention to the study of problems connected with water pollution. He will then be able to devote an increasing amount of time to planning in the form of a general appraisal of the state of water resources. This is a logical development; after efforts have been made to clean up sources of pollution, the next step is to turn to a rational control of water management. It is expected that progressively greater demands will be made on the ability of hydrologists to describe hydrological processes in such a way that this knowledge can be integrated with the general approach.

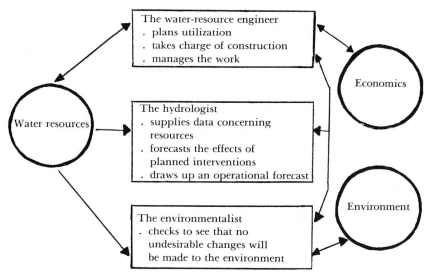

Utilization of water resources demands close cooperation by various experts.

The modern water-resource engineer collaborates with the hydrologist in solving water problems, not only in Sweden but in other countries as well, not least in the developing countries. Swedish engineering firms are already taking part in a series of water projects in India, Africa (Tanzania, Kenya, Ethiopia, Botswana, etc.), South America, and elsewhere. Swedish activities have also attracted considerable interest in other industrialized countries, e.g., Japan and Australia. Particular interest has been focused on activities in the developing countries.

As a rule, one of the prime tasks in these countries is treatment of water. Domestic consumption is usually extremely low, and it is not uncommon for the well from which a family draws its water to be situated several kilometers away from the home. Watercourses are often polluted because of inadequate standards of livestock hygiene, with

163

the result that waterborne diseases are common. One of the essential tasks of the engineer-hydrologist is, therefore, to find suitable alternative sources of water supply, and this can be a time-consuming process, due among other things to the absence of hydrological data. Once the primary needs concerning water supply have been provided for, hydrological data are needed for the drawing up of plans for more comprehensive water supply arrangements covering wider areas. Unfortunately, the engineer is often at a disadvantage here, because he starts in a situation where water demand is not satisfied and has to expand the system to meet the needs of a population which is rising steeply in number.

Many of the difficulties confronting the engineer are bound up with demands which have nothing to do with the actual business of water management—demands of a political, economic, and religious nature, for instance. The last-mentioned of these may include prejudice against the introduction of new methods. Many such prejudices are reflected by irrigation techniques, and some of them may be connected with previous failures by experts from the industrialized countries.

A great deal remains to be done, particularly in the context of irrigation, and the idea of a Swedish research station in Africa, which has been put forward by Swedish engineers, might be a source of benefit to Africans and to the efforts being made by Swedes in the developing countries. It is also important to note in this context that the training of Swedish engineers and hydrologists needs to be improved on their home ground so that they are better equipped to elucidate and deal sympathetically with the problems of the developing countries. Irrigation and groundwater problems are among those deserving special attention.

Swedish investigations in India have shown the need for a thorough knowledge of groundwater exploitation. Many mistakes have been made in this sector, including the mistake of heavy extraction without previous investigation of the means, if any, whereby reserves of groundwater are replenished. In some dry zones of the developing countries this can lead ultimately to the intrusion of saline water. As a result, it is not uncommon for these wells and irrigation works to have to be abandoned.

Rational water management in industry

There are also other sectors in which Swedish engineering, acting in collaboration with other types of expertise—the natural sciences, for instance—has helped to bring about a rational utilization of our water resources. It is particularly interesting to note the methods which are being developed to save water in industry. Measures of this kind have been successfully adopted in the iron and steel sector. One of the characteristics of these industries is that a great deal of the water they need is for the transportation of heavy materials. The water does not have to be of particularly good quality, which means that recycling is a feasible proposition. The steel industry normally consumes 250 l of water per kg of finished steel. Steelworks in those parts of Europe where water resources are under the heaviest strain have been able to bring down the water requirement in crude steel manufacturing to about 5 1/kg, which means a tremendous saving.

Mining is another industry where there is scope for economy in the use of water. Efforts are being made in this sector to adopt systems which are as self-contained as possible. Hematite, a reddish-colored iron ore, is a particularly troublesome pollutant. Not only does it color rivers, but the fine particles of the ore have properties which make it hard to precipitate. Methods have been evolved whereby the water can be recycled following a purification process.

The paper and pulp industry is yet another sector where efforts are being made to devise means of recycling the water after use in the production process. This industry has long had the reputation of being one of the largest consumers and polluters of water. It is of no mean importance that efforts should be made to develop new processing techniques whereby water can be recycled. Paper and pulp manufacturing accounts for no less than 80 percent of the total amount of water used by industry in Sweden. The largest quantities of water in the industry are used for the bleaching processes. Different paper products involve very different amounts of water. Process water consumption for the manufacture of newsprint can be kept as low as 10 m³ per ton of finished product. But there are other grades which cannot be produced with such small quantities of water. The manufacture of cable paper is one such example. Good cable paper can be manufactured only by keeping the salt content to a minimum. This makes it difficult for cable paper to be manufactured in a self-contained system, because salt accumulates in the process water.

Thus, there are several fields in which the hydrologist, the water-resource engineer, and the environmentalist together can devise methods to reduce the amount of pollution and save water in industry. Together these three experts can help to solve the water problems of the developing countries by contributing the hydrological and technical knowledge which is essential.

Water management is quite possible

This was the idea with which we began this chapter. One may now ask whether or not the chapter has proved the point. The answer can be given as follows: We have shown that there is a very large international organization which has worked for ten years (1965-74) to make an inventory of the world's water resources and to provide guidance for the proper management of those resources. We have also noted that these IHD activities have been succeeded by the activities of the IHP. One of the aims of the latter continues to be making an inventory and analysis of the world's water resources, but another important task has been added, namely that of studying the repercussions which human influence can be expected to have on the various components of the hydrological cycle. The IHP is a manifestation of global awareness and responsibility concerning the vital questions arising from the management of water as a limited resource.

166

This chapter also included a description of some of the methods used by hydrologists and other water scientists to solve difficult quantitative and qualitative problems of water management. We also considered practical examples of the work done by hydrologists and water-resource engineers in solving global problems of water supply. Finally, we described the efforts being made, particularly in the industrial sector, to reduce the water demand. Here, as in other sectors, the need is for innovation.

One is entitled to conclude that rational management of our water resources is within the bounds of possibility, but perhaps most important of all will be comprehensive planning to be carried out in time, whether or not we have an abundance of water today. *Nobody will have plenty of water tomorrow. When tomorrow comes, we must be able to manage and plan so that we can help each other by global consensus.*

9   *The key role of knowledge transfer*

The vital function of information transfer

In the preceding chapters we have considered a series of problems, all of which reflect the role of water in human life. The most fundamental of these have concerned the constellation of population, food, and water. Bearing in mind that by the end of this century the earth's population will be twice what it is today, we have also touched on the enormous development of irrigation which will be needed in the relatively dry areas inhabited by most of the human race. The forecasts which have been drawn up for the year 2000 indicate the need to provide three times as much water for the human community as is being provided today, and that the greater part of this will be for irrigation purposes.

The rising population will generate enormous pollution problems unless a new water policy is implemented. There is good reason to suppose that by the year 2000 more than half the population of the world will be living in urban communities. Man is becoming more and more an urban animal. In 1950, there were about seventy-five cities each with over a million inhabitants. By the year 2000 there are expected to be 275. By that time it is estimated that 80 percent of the inhabitants of the industrialized countries and 40 percent of the inhabitants of the developing countries will be living in urban areas. In hard figures, this implies an increase of 2 billion in the urban population of the world, with 450 million new urban residents in the industrialized countries and 1 billion in the developing countries. It is worth adding that, between 1970 and 1985 alone, Bandung is expected to increase its population by 242 percent, Lagos by 186 percent, Bogota and Baghdad by about 145 percent each.

This shift of population from rural to urban areas is

bound to give rise to the problems of supply which we have indicated. It is equally self-evident that information and the transfer of knowledge concerning water questions will occupy a key role in the water development process connected with this changing human situation, a situation which must lead to a wiser and more responsible use of the water resources of industrialized and developing countries alike.

We know that international development is a protracted endeavor aimed at enabling the developing countries to fend for themselves, the idea being for development to come from within. The efficacy of international assistance is therefore limited by the ability of the recipient country to accept innovations and adjust them to its own needs. External help will of course have a stimulating effect on this process. The assistance given by industrialized countries in the form of knowledge needs time to be assimilated by the recipient. Only when this has been accomplished can the transfer of knowledge take full effect. In this way the transfer of knowledge is one of the most effective forms of international assistance, because it increases the number of persons capable of handling innovative ideas and material assistance.

The interaction of transmitter and receiver

A process of knowledge transfer involves two or more parties. There is always an active party, whom we may term the transmitter or the source of knowledge, and there is the receiver of the knowledge. There is also a certain amount of feedback in the form of information from the receiver to the source. A constructive transfer of knowledge—from industrialized to developing countries, for example—must be founded on feedback from the recipient, who may have to tell the transmitter that this or that method cannot be practised, owing to local conditions which may not have been known when the process of knowledge transfer began.

The knowledge-transfer process is an important social

task. It is fair to say that development and progress will be dependent on the facilities established for the communication of information concerning the advances of science and technology. We have no reason to suppose that this process of advance in the various research sectors will come to a halt. Politicians and national and international organizations therefore have a growing duty to ensure that the transfer of knowledge can proceed efficiently.

In this chapter, we shall consider some of the problems of knowledge transfer which can occur in the water sector. Here, as in other contexts, there are certain important groupings, such as industrialized and developing countries, scientists and practitioners, scientists and the general public, and so on.

The dangerous aversion to experts

History teaches us that people trying to speed up the flow of knowledge invariably meet with difficulties. Active resistance, of course, is the greatest adversary, coming as it does on top of all the other difficulties with which the process has to contend. This active resistance includes among other things the antiscientific movements which crop up every now and then and which are enjoying a certain prosperity today. The breeding ground of these movements is the feeling that scientific development has damaged our environment, that science and technology generate power, and so on. To repulse these attacks on a development and transfer of knowledge, which is indispensable to the general course of development, we must penetrate and analyze in greater depth the processes by which the transfer of knowledge is governed. We have to identify the shortcomings of this process so that, by constantly endeavoring to correct mistakes, we can make the transfer of knowledge as efficient as possible.

Knowledge transfer is an active process in itself, but we also have to find the mainspring of this activity. When considering the transfer of knowledge in the water sector, between industrialized and developing countries, knowledge requirements are in a manner of speaking governed by and coordinated with activities in other sectors. Knowledge transfer in the water sector is therefore liable to be a time-consuming, complex task involving a struggle against difficulties which are not always referable to problems within the water sector itself.

Knowledge is transformed on its way from transmitter to receiver

Knowledge transfer is a complex process. A measure of simplification and schematization is therefore appropriate. We said that knowledge transfer requires a transmitter and a receiver. The general pattern also includes a mediator of knowledge, who may be said to constitute a link in the transfer process. This link plays a vital part in the entire transfer process, because it governs the knowledge transferred. The link is often compared to a filter, because it filters off part of the knowledge originally bound from the transmitter to the receiver. In this way a certain amount of information is lost or cut off, frequently quite unintentionally. The information processed by the mediator is recast or processed before it goes any further, with the result that the original amount of knowledge is reduced. Similarly, a certain filtration effect occurs along the information search route in the opposite direction, i.e., from receiver to transmitter.

It is important to make clear that the filtration process described here is not necessarily confined to the reduction of knowledge, nor is this the intention. On the contrary, the task of the filter may be a positive one. One need only consider the occasions when data emitted by the source may need to be sifted, for instance, prior to the transmission of information to the general public.

An example

Knowledge transfer can be illustrated in simple terms by a

diagram such as that shown on page 173. In that diagram we have chosen the example of a firm of consulting engineers which has to plan an exceedingly comprehensive water supply system. The firm realizes that certain difficult subsidiary problems may be involved, due perhaps to lack of documentation. And even if the necessary documentation is available at the beginning of the project, it is still uncertain whether or not the engineers will be able to solve these problems, because this may demand a special kind of knowledge which is lacking.

A specialist in this sector is therefore consulted. We have termed the two parties "practitioner" and "scientist" respectively, and accordingly their respective roles will be termed "practical function" and "scientific function." Our analysis of the interaction between these two can start in the diagram square marked "planning, operation, and development." The firm of engineers asks if there are any subsidiary problems which it is unable to solve, or if there are any unanswered questions limiting an optimum solution which, for instance, might have to be presented to a political decisionmaker. If the answer to these questions is negative, we proceed via the arrows in the diagram to the square marked "carry on with the project." If, on the other hand, there are problems, we follow the "Yes" arrow, which leads to a square marked "identification and definition of the research task."

This means that the problem which could not be solved and which one would like the research institution to solve one way or another, has to be defined. The question now is whether the assignment can be formulated without losing certain basic information in the process, thereby causing the institution to misinterpret its task. In other words, how will the research institution understand the task which is presented to it? The term "filter" is used here to symbolize the knowledge and information which disappear. There is, therefore, some danger of the problems studied under the research assignment not being completely identical with the problems which should have been studied. This, of course, is liable to affect the work done subsequently

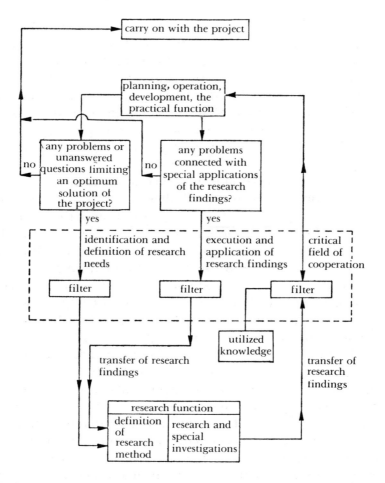

Explanatory diagram to show the channels of communication between the research function and the practical function.

by the firm of engineers. The research institution now formulates a method whereby it intends to solve the problem and it enumerates the special investigation which it believes will be necessary.

The expert must express himself clearly

After these investigations have been completed, the results

are presented: this is termed "transfer of research findings" in the diagram. Here again, a filter is present. Knowledge is reduced because of the scientist's inability to present his results in such a way that they can be fully understood and correctly applied to the water supply problems confronting the firm of engineers. Misunderstandings can result in a residue of "unutilized knowledge." Another possible reason for this residue is that research reports are left unread on the recipient's desk.

The new information is now fed into the firm's activities. Once again, the firm asks if there are any problems or unanswered questions limiting the solution of the problem in spite of the new information which has been supplied. If there are not, the firm can carry on with the project. If there are—for instance, problems may arise concerning special applications of the solicited research findings—the transfer process is repeated, with new information being requested from the research institutions. This too involves the risk of a reduction of the mass of knowledge.

The filter effect indicated here is not to be underrated. It may be due to practitioner and scientist having different frames of reference, so that they tend to talk at cross purposes. There may be perfectly natural reasons for this: they may be differently educated, they may employ different terminology, or they may be inarticulate. Most people have doubtless found themselves in similar situations at one time or another, for example, when receiving information via mass media such as newspapers, radio, or television.

Irrigation has to be learned by the individual peasant in the developing countries

After our simplified analysis of the possible course of knowledge transfer, we can turn to consider some concrete examples of the interaction, or lack of interaction, accompanying transfer of knowledge between industrialized and developing countries. What could be more natural than to consider the problem of knowledge transfer with reference to

174

irrigation? We have already remarked on the indispensability of irrigation in farming, particularly in the developing countries. Irrigation being the largest item of total water use, it is essential for water to be managed in such a way as to give an optimum return in plant cultivation. One of the principal weaknesses of the knowledge transfer system is that information fails to reach the recipient in a manner conducive to its implementation.

A great deal of attention needs to be focused on "the forgotten man" who, ultimately, has to apply the knowledge to achieve a higher agricultural output. Irrigation was once an "art," and in countries like China and Egypt it is as ancient as civilization itself. In an age of slow population growth, techniques which had evolved through the accumulation of experience were sufficient to meet the demands placed on agriculture. Today, rapidly rising food demand calls for advanced technology of a completely different order.

In the majority of developing countries it is not known how much water needs to be supplied in order to irrigate a field, nor is it known when and how often irrigation should be practised in order to maximize crop yields. Today the ratio between water consumption and crop yield can often be 5,000 tons of water per ton of wheat and 15,000-20,000 tons of water per ton of rice. It is believed, however, that better management, better fertilization, and better seed should make it possible for these ratios to be reduced to one-fifth, i.e., to 1,000 tons for wheat and 3,000 tons for rice. It is fairly easy to convince the farmer of the advantages of soil improvement or of high-yield varieties. It is less easy to demonstrate the advantages of improved water management, especially as the methods advocated may often conflict with local irrigation practises evolved over the centuries, or traditions concerning the management of rain-fed agriculture.

Salinization and waterlogging bear eloquent witness to an insufficient transfer of knowledge

Conflicts can also be provoked by the indiscreet application of the methods of the industrialized countries to farming in the developing countries. The knowledge and experience of the industrialized countries are not always directly applicable to a developing country; sometimes they have to be modified according to differences of climate, geology, etc. Every situation has to be judged separately with due regard to local infrastructure, history, and culture; otherwise, mistakes are liable to occur, resulting in the salinization and waterlogging of the soil. It will be recalled from chapter 3 that the former is due to salt remaining and accumulating in the upper layer of the soil as a result of evaporation, while the latter is due to excessively copious irrigation. Most of the surplus water administered through excessive irrigation seeps through the soil, causing the water table to rise gradually, until in the end the entire area may be underwater.

It will also be recalled that the extent of salinization and waterlogging of arable land has resulted from a failure to apply the knowledge which we already possess. This knowledge has failed to reach decisionmakers and practitioners.

The negative consequences of irrigation have be overcome

Irrigation can also result in damage other than salinization and waterlogging. In some instances the need to expand irrigated acreage and raise food production has led to the depletion of groundwater reservoirs in certain areas. Too much water has been extracted and insufficient thought given to the absence of natural replenishment of these resources. This has happened in Saudi Arabia, Israel, South Africa, Texas, Arizona, and southern California, India, and many other parts of the world. In cases of this kind, a shortlived rise in production is liable to be followed by a distinct fall in crop yields.

A great deal of chapter 3 was concerned with the consequences of irrigation, correctly or otherwise organized, the purpose being to indicate some of the difficulties which have to be overcome in order to raise the agricultural output of our starving world. We also found that the estimated "profit" on an irrigation enterprise can easily turn into a "loss" when account is also had of the ecological and biological repercussions which may follow. We have just mentioned the importance of paying due regard to the many factors that determine which methods are suitable, and to the idiosyncrasies of the country or region from the point of view of production. These factors are never static; they change generally with the ongoing process of development. For this reason, both the type of knowledge and the manner of its transfer should be reviewed regularly.

FAO, the international organization whose main task is to fight malnutrition, hunger, and poverty, has given top priority to, transfer of knowledge. Vehicles for transfer include seminars, regional research activities, panels of experts, working committees and consultants, publications, and UN-financed technical assistance, projects, consultative assistance, and scholarships. To make the transfer process as efficient as possible, FAO attaches great importance to the careful selection and preparation of the persons who are to act as intermediaries and of those who are primarily to receive and apply the knowledge.

Numerous barriers between developed and developing countries

A well-known expert on the developing countries—Aaron Wiener—has said that technological information is easier to transfer than the capacity for making decisions. He remarks that inexperienced professionals in the developing countries are often ill-equipped for taking of big and important decisions. Key positions and senior appointments in the decision-making process are usually held by young people whose personal qualifications are often insufficient for them to be able to respond to the forces of development.

There are three major pitfalls in the transfer of knowledge in the water sciences to the developing countries. The first

177

difficulty is that the knowledge to be transferred from an industrialized to a developing country is often limited to a relatively narrow sector, whereas underdevelopment covers a multitude of sectors and the transfer of knowledge within a single sector has repercussions on a wider pattern of socio-economic sectors. Transfer, therefore, demands planning and methodology covering a relatively wide field. The second difficulty lies in the fact that the methods which an industrialized country can apply to the solution of its technical problems are not necessarily appropriate to the solution of problems in the developing countries. In a developing country, the need is for a planning process embracing several levels, not the one-sided approach to the solution of problems which has characterized many water projects in the industrialized countries to date. The third mistake is that transfer often refers to problem-solving routines which are inappropriate to the often unusual conditions found in many developing countries.

We could therefore do with a new set of tools, tools which are far more sensitive to the situations applying in the Third World. Wiener proposes a thorough redeployment of international assistance activities in favor of a knowledge transfer having the following activities as its nucleus: pilot projects aimed at securing important information and training local work teams, and full-scale projects by the continuous re-training and remotivation of skilled personnel. He also proposes that resource utilization be planned with regard to more sectors of social development in such a way that projects are selected which actually lead to the achievement of concrete goals of development.

In our general analysis of the transfer of knowledge, we had occasion to refer to filters. We could equally well have called them barriers. There are any number of barriers in the way of transfers between industrialized and developing countries. Not only are there national boundaries of language, technology, economics, social, cultural, and political conditions, there are also differences of climate, geology, topography, and demography. All of these differences help to create very distinct barriers.

The public must be better informed

The general public is a neglected recipient group where information in the water sector is concerned; the information issued today is now very wide and often has a heavy sectorial bias. For a long time, the bulk of information has centered on questions concerning water quality. On the other hand, the water sector should be an extremely rewarding field. The recipient party has no difficulty in experiencing motivation, because every individual comes into daily contact with the hydrological cycle both in its natural state—rain, snow, lakes, rivers—and in the course of its application to everyday life—water supply, laundry, garden watering, etc. The flow of groundwater beneath the ground on which we walk is a subject that fascinates most people.

At the same time, the water sector would seem to be one of the sectors where "witchcraft" is elevated to a system: the persistent survival of the water diviner is a direct consequence of unsatisfactory knowledge transfer. It also holds a powerful attraction for the mass media, thus diverting attention from empirical information about groundwater flows.

The importance of the man-in-the-street being given objective and balanced information concerning the natural hydrological system, and the human relations with it, is obvious. Only when such information is readily available will current events be viewed in their proper perspective and informed opinion brought to bear on political decision-making and priorities.

The general public has several difficulties to contend with. The flow of information is too narrow to give a comprehensive picture, and filters intervene in the form of popularization. The knowledge of the intermediary group (the link) is often limited. All this leads to distortion, often to tendentious misrepresenataion. The narrow frames of reference of the recipient group and its consequent difficulties in interpreting (understanding) the information received is a barrier due to school instruction not having provided more than a very elementary description of the hydrological cycle.

Consequently, the recipient's interpretation is to a great extent determined by his own sphere of direct experience (observations around his holiday home in the country, childhood memories, etc.).

The difficulties of reaching the public

There are several possible channels available for the transfer of information about water. First and foremost, there is the audiovisual channel via films and TV broadcasts. A filter effect occurs here, however, due to various shortcomings in the knowledge possessed by the film maker and the program producer. They, in turn, are dependent on written information transfer by popular scientific literature of different kinds. The books on continental water are still relatively few in number, and the overwhelming majority of articles in technical journals deal with the water quality sector without doing very much to relate it to the dynamics of the hydrological cycle. Oral information transfer through interviews, lectures, and courses provides another important channel, but the information which can be transferred via this channel is obviously limited.

One barrier which is not to be understood is the habit of oversimplifying written information brought about by comic strips. Because of this barrier, even groups in search of information may be averse to information conveyed by the printed word. An example was provided by the general and global hydrological exhibition produced by Swedish Travelling Exhibitions a few years ago in the form of eleven screens. In constructing this exhibition, every effort was made to reduce the accompanying text on the screens to an absolute minimum, and yet the exhibition was heavily criticized for containing too much printed text! It is, of course, impossible for any complex information to be communicated through an exhibition without the aid of printed text; pictures of complex relationships and processes cannot be made sufficiently informative, especially when the fundamental frames of reference are, to a great extent, lacking among the visiting public.

To many people, the daily newspapers are the most important route of knowledge transfer, and newspapers have a very important part to play in transferring of knowledge concerning water. But the interest taken by newspapers in broadening the information they supply on technical and scientific questions often falls far short of the importance of these sectors of reality to the general public. Even the largest daily newspapers have only a handful of journalists to cover the technical and environmental sectors. They do great work and are often highly dedicated, but their numbers are so small that they cannot be expected to accomplish very much in our field of interest.

All the difficulties mentioned here concerning the transfer of information between scientists and the general public appear to result in a certain distrust of scientific research; the somewhat uncritical manner in which new findings are presented and the mutual contradictions of different findings give the general public the impression that scientists are not to be relied on because no two scientists agree. It is not realized that this is the way research operates, and too extensive interpretation is sometimes put on isolated research findings. Newspaper headlines with their breathtaking simplifications of fact are another serious problem, because quite often a headline travesties the information conveyed by the article.

A proper information link is urgently needed between scientists and the general public to inform the latter about the water problems which lie ahead. What we lack is a complete *professional corps of information mediators,* whose task is to transform technical and scientific information by different media and in various forms, so that the general public is provided with the information to which it is entitled.

Knowledge transfer—when, where, and how?

Returning to the special problems of knowledge transfer in .

the water-resource sector, we can summarize them in a series of questions which, unfortunately, are not easily answered:

1. What hydrological knowledge should be transferred?
2. How is this knowledge to be transferred, i.e., what particular methods are likely to produce the most effective transfer?
3. Who is to communicate this knowledge, or what persons or institutions can be considered best qualified for the task of transferring the knowledge?
4. At what juncture should knowledge be transferred in order to make specific water information as effective as possible in view of the dissemination of interfering knowledge which occurs in neighboring sectors?
5. Why should knowledge be transferred, and what further goals can be attained by improving the knowledge of the individual citizen, society in general, etc.?

How to obtain a more effective transfer of knowledge

As we saw earlier, the link which communicates knowledge from the source to the recipient is an extremely important factor. Bilateral and international bodies are profoundly committed as links in the transfer of knowledge between industrialized and developing countries. The transfer is at present administered by experts from the developing countries who have been trained in the industrialized countries by experts serving as consultants, and through the medium of symposia and courses held in the developing countries. Between scientists and practitioners, a link should be created in the form of a body for the analysis of information, in which critical but practically oriented reporters would be charged with checking and streamlining the scientific information coming from researchers, reducing the mass of information while preserving its scientific quality, and elucidating possible fields of application where research findings are of practical importance. The link between scientific research and the general public needs to be expanded by means of *research information journalists,* i.e., hydrologists who are also trained journalists.

It is through links of these kinds that the questions stated above need to be handled. The link should be able to decide what knowledge is to be passed on, how this can best be done and when it can best be done. To satisfy the requirements, it is essential that the links be staffed by specially trained hydrological experts. In view of the exponential growth of scientific publications, it will very soon be time to acknowledge that direct contact between scientist and practitioner can no longer provide the full amount of information transfer needed between the two groups. Nor is it realistic to demand that a consulting engineer should devote more of his time than he already does today to keeping up with a growing, and in some respects increasingly theoretical and complex, literature in the field of water science.

There are many sectors where developments are liable to move us to despair, and the hydrological sector is not lacking in examples. One such example shows how deforestation on mountain slopes causes erosion due to the ease with which rainfall can wash away material from the cleared area when the protective cover of vegetation is removed. This phenomenon is not new; Plato described it about twenty-five centuries ago! Almost four hundred years ago, the Frenchman Bernard Palissy explained that terracing was the only feasible method of farming on steeply sloping ground. Yet in India, Kenya, the Philippines, Indonesia, and other places these simple rules are broken. Here as everywhere else in the hydrological sector—a field of vital importance to the future of mankind—great and momentous tasks remain to be done in this age of exploding populations. We must take up the fight against ignorance wherever it holds sway.

The transfer problems of our age are not merely due to our being inundated by a rapidly growing output of knowledge, some of which confuses us because it is no more than a reiteration in new guise of knowledge that is already established. Instead the problem is one of quality, which in turn is connected with the defects of the pattern of knowledge transfer. The problem is not that the channels of knowledge transfer are overburdened with useless and outmoded traffic. Instead, our problem lies in the reconstruction and creation of a more efficient transfer network. The world is growing smaller and smaller as a result of the various communication networks established by modern technology; at the same time mutual global problems are getting bigger and bigger. We, therefore, have to find a new and qualitatively superior pattern of communication which will provide the greater efficiency that knowledge transfer now demands.

10   *Epilogue*

Taking stock

Water is a natural resource which will exist forever; it cannot be depleted, because it is renewable. Nor can water be replaced in the way that the non-renewable resources of our world will have to be sooner or later by substitutes. Water will always be an essential ingredient of life itself.

The steep rise in water demand and water utilization which has recently begun is now in the process of generating global problems. We do not yet know what repercussions the steep rise in plant production, achieved by irrigation, will have on the hydrological cycle. Very considerable flows of water will be diverted into the atmosphere by evaporation from irrigated fields. If even more water is diverted into the atmosphere, river discharge into the sea will be reduced correspondingly. What will then happen to the sea level and to our climate? There are other ways in which human activity interferes with the hydrological cycle: deforestation and urbanization are two important examples of indirect influence. Direct interference with rivers and groundwater also has ecological repercussions. The aggregate effect of all these consequences may be solvable only on a global basis by international cooperation.

The annual runoff into rivers and groundwater constitutes the water resource from which man has to provide for his water requirements. As far as can be foreseen today, water resources are adequate for human needs, but considerable changes will have to be made to current water policy if we are to avoid being "swamped" in the rising tide of waste water. Treatment will not get us very far. If the concentration of pollutants in waste water is cut to a third at the same time as the volume of waste water is trebled, the amount of pollution carried by the water will remain the same. Industry must, therefore, reduce its water demand by means of alternative technology. Dry manufacturing processes will have to be used more frequently. Indispensable water must be recycled, and water which cannot be recycled must undergo advanced purification before being returned to rivers.

Water is a key element in the improvement of agricultural output. It has to be applied in suitable quantities, at the right time, and through well-managed irrigation works. Many poor countries are poor because they are situated in arid zones where the shortage of water is a fundamental obstacle to efficient farming. Drought, which has affected many regions of the world recently, is a condition imposed by nature upon those who wish to live in these zones, and it has to be counterbalanced by irrigation. But the establishment of the requisite irrigation works will involve a great deal of investment in the form of capital and labor and will require a great deal of international cooperation and generosity.

Prior to the UN World Food Conference in Rome, FAO estimated that to repair dilapidated irrigation works and build the new ones judged necessary during the coming ten years would cost a total of $60 billion. Of this amount, it is expected that a considerable proportion can be covered by the input of native labor, but the necessary external financing for the coming ten-year period is estimated at about $2 billion per annum. By way of comparison, Swedish hydrological assistance today corresponds to about $10 million per annum.

Under optimum production conditions, the world's total cultivable area would be perfectly sufficient to keep the entire population of the world well fed and properly nourished throughout the foreseeable future. But some continents will never become self-sufficient, because all their fertile land is already under cultivation. The paramount problems of agriculture in the arid zones today, namely salinization and waterlogging, must be solved quickly. The solution of these problems is a necessary condition of the development of irrigated farming in the arid zones. This does not call for research, but for the application of existing knowledge. Irrigation will also have to be paralleled by a general improvement in farming techniques.

Comprehensive and well-integrated water management is of crucial importance to the future water supplies of mankind and to the water conservation which must be steadfastly conducted on a global scale.

Water is unevenly distributed in time and space in all the continents of the world. Some areas are short of water; others have too much. At certain times of the year large areas are inundated; at other times human beings, plant life, and animals are paralyzed by drought. These inequalities in the available supply will have to be evened out. This can be done by diverting water from surplus to deficit areas, or by storing water from the rainy season of the year for use later on, after a river has dried up.

Human interference with the hydrological cycle must be kept under control to save the natural system from dissolving into chaos. Given the determination, this should be perfectly feasible in an age when man is capable of flying to the moon. Some of the implements of this control are very ancient indeed. The Chinese were building dams more than 2,000 years ago, the Greeks had tunnels and conduits 2,500 years ago, and irrigation was being practised 5,000 years ago in ancient Egypt. Irrigation was the factor which forced the inhabitants of these river areas to join together in civilizations. The novelty of our situation, however, lies in its format and in the availability of the computer to those who have to wrestle with intricate and complex relationships, and with the many complicated calculations that have to be made to cater to many simultaneous and conflicting demands on water.

Not all cultivable land in these dry zones is within reach of a river. Even if maximum use were to be made of every major desert river, great areas of desert would remain untouched. Large and important installations are already being planned in the Nile and the Indus, in the Tigris and Euphrates valleys, in the Orange River in South Africa, and in the Colorado and Columbia Rivers in the United States. No major desert river is unutilized today. For the rest, one has to depend on artificial systems of water transfer. As most of the earth's deserts have no natural means of water transfer, grandiose conduit systems will have to be constructed to bring water from remote areas which have surpluses. Discussions concerning a gigantic project of this kind have started under the aegis of NAWAPA. Other discussions are taking place about the utilization of the Siberian rivers and the great Central African reservoir of Lake Chad. At present, however, undertakings on this scale appear to be beyond the resources even of such affluent and well-educated countries as the United States and the USSR.

Water-transfer and water-control projects often cause political problems, such as between India and Pakistan concerning the water of the Indus system, and between the various countries with stakes in the Mekong River. International cooperation must be expanded to establish the necessary control and a fair allocation of river water and groundwater.

The grandiloquent proposals for the control of water will also cost a great deal of money and divert labor and expertise that would be used elsewhere. Big interests are becoming involved, and new political constellations are emerging. In a different situation the Aswam Dam could have been financed by Britain and the United States, but the wind changed and the decisive interest was shown by the USSR, which could have used the resources for its own desert irrigation project.

The environmentalists of the future

Completely new perspectives are opened up where nature conservancy and environmental influence are concerned. The development of a more reasonable water supply in thirsty parts of the world calls for extensive interference with the natural hydrological cycle. Water *must* be transferred from the places where it is available to the places where it forms a necessary ingredient of human life. Water transfer projects are, therefore, destined to become very common. However, water *must* be stored on a very large scale during rainy periods for use in dry periods. Innumerable reservoirs will have to be constructed both above and below ground, the latter requiring the development of a new technology.

Environmentalist groups in the developed countries of the world appear to be divided. The preservationists want to keep nature as it is and prevent interference and redeployments. The conservationists, on the other hand, are prepared to countenance interference so long as it is defensible, but are also prepared to make great efforts to restrain the negative effects on the environment.

It is clear that the developments now taking shape to provide the world's future supplies of water leave less scope for the first of these two schools, whose philosophy would rapidly lead to widespread death by starvation. Instead, the conservationists must be given an opportunity to become profoundly involved in the development process. They must create the public opinion to demand the thorough investigation of every water resource project with regard to its possible repercussions on the external environment and to the incorporation in the project, from its very beginning, of countermeasures against negative consequences. This kind of attitude combined with the utilization of knowledge already available would, for example, make it possible to avoid the continuing salinization of irrigated land, which, as we saw in a previous chapter, has an unsuspectedly widespread effect on people living in dry zones.

How can we avoid new errors?

For large areas of the world, only very rough estimates of water resources are available. The basic figures of total river discharge, which constitutes mankind's total water resources, are still very uncertain. The fact is that the first measurement of the flow of the Amazon, which was undertaken in the mid-1960s, led to a considerable modification of estimated total global runoff. Whereas previously the Amazon had been thought to account for 11 percent of total river discharge, it now transpired that 18 percent was a more credible figure. Obviously, the advanced water planning and water management, without which the future water requirements of a growing world population cannot be met, will demand the establishment of a comprehensive and well-planned hydrological observation network capable of producing accurate measurements of water resources. We also need to know more about the circulation of water in the natural system, the interaction of quantity and quality, and hydrological and ecological factors.

In view of the international character of the global circulation system, international cooperation will be indispensible for studies of the world's water resources. Cooperation of this kind began to be effective between 1965 and 1974 under the aegis of the International Hydrological Decade (IHD), in which 107 countries took part. At the beginning of 1975, this cooperation was placed on a permanent footing through the institution of a follow-up project, the International Hydrological Programme (IHP), also sponsored by UNESCO. Obviously, it is of fundamental importance for these efforts to be given the powerful support of all the countries of the world, both nationally and internationally. Water supply can no longer be regarded as a pure and simple technical matter.

Repetition of previous mistakes can be avoided if action is based on wider ranging knowledge, which it will be the task of scientific research to accumulate systematically. Not that different problems and relationships are to be viewed in isolation. We must feel our way towards the order existing between the elements that make up our world—natural elements, social elements, and the technological elements added by man. C.A. Doxiadis, the Greek world-community scientist of the School of Ekistics in Athens, has started one such experiment. He regards life on earth as being made up of five elements: nature, man, society, shell (buildings and constructions), and network systems (conduits and communications). These five elements require more than 200 components in order for their main features to be described.

190

Paired relations can be sought between any of these components.

It will be necessary in the future for the system of life to be viewed like this, as an integral whole. We cannot continue to view our problems singly. We cannot—as if plucking the leaves of an artichoke—rectify them one at a time as has been the practise so far in human history. In urban development, for example, we have concentrated on one area after another but seldom on several areas together. Doxiadis points out that in the course of fifty years man has gradually changed his spheres of interest in the following order: buildings, communications, social conditions, and nature and the environment. Now that we are turning to the negative effects on our environment, we immediately stumble, for example, on social conditions in the form of unemployment which are liable to happen if industrial antipollution costs become too high. We purchase our employment at the price of continued destruction of the quality of our water.

In future developments which are inescapable within the water sector, the transfer of knowledge will present a task of formidable dimensions. The knowledge of how water is to be handled must reach all the way to the peasant whose field is to be watered. He is the key figure in development, and without his cooperation the necessary food output will be unattainable.

Other obstacles to be surmounted

There are also a number of human obstacles to be negotiated. These include a series of institutional and organizational pitfalls, such as the allocation of responsibility and differences concerning priorities, where several nations are involved. National bodies include special development authorities often set up to cover a particular river zone.

International water legislation is inadequate. Practically all major rivers are shared by two or more countries, and innumerable international agreements will have to be concluded during the next few decades. Problems of national legislation include the inadequacy of legislation in former colonial countries, based as it is on the traditions of mother countries with very different water resources. The establishment of legislative and legal awareness in the people is another important issue.

Economic and financial factors are fundamental. Where is all the money needed for the development of water resources to be found? Clearly, there will have to be a massive diversion of finance from the satellite and military sectors to food production. Are priorities within major projects to be determined by the budget-makers themselves? Financial difficulties constitute one of the greatest dilemmas of river-administration authorities today. How great a contribution is expected from individuals on the other side of the property fence in order for a project to succeed? Do they have sufficient motivation for this purpose? Land ownership is another stumbling block, especially the discrepancy between the interests of magnates and those of small landowners.

Population development is often so rapid that a source of water supply may be inadequate by the time it is completed. Interest and motivation are two essential factors, and they, in turn, are related to willingness or unwillingness to accept innovations. Which person in a village is to be encouraged to run his farm on more modern lines—the richest and most successful villager, or the poorest who does not stand to lose very much by the initial hostility of his neighbors?

As we have already observed, the question of knowledge and information is also vitally important. No sensible project can be planned without reliable basic information. This is a question of necessary insight into the detailed functioning of the natural hydrological cycle in the particular area, and of access to basic observation data for a long enough period. Precipitation and river discharge data are needed for much more than ten years in order for conclusions to be drawn concerning flood or drought risks. For instance, the recent drought in the Sahel zone was of a kind occurring at fifty-year intervals.

Social and cultural factors are of the utmost importance. Can a cooperative spirit be instilled among neighboring peoples? What are their customs and which of these customs can be conditioned?

The UN World Water Conference

As we have now seen, water impinges on human life in innumerable ways. As a society develops, the interaction between the human community and natural water supply becomes more and more complex. The interaction between water management and the functioning of society is abundantly illustrated by a society like Egypt, where the mutual relationship between the country's inhabitants and the Nile is the very nucleus of the social structure, and where since time immemorial life has followed the rhythm of the river. Clearly, the change to a more modern system of water management and irrigation entails vast upheavals of such a community's social life.

Despite the manifold use of and dependence on water resources, we have seen that our society has not assimilated the knowledge which scientists have accumulated; many of the various hydrological mishaps we encounter could have been greatly alleviated or even avoided if the decision makers had had better access to existing knowledge concerning the role of water in the natural environment, and if they had been in a position to translate that knowledge into practical policy. The surprisingly poor adjustment of human life to current elementary climatic and hydrologic conditions is a case in point. Instead of adapting their sophisticated communities to the fluctuations between wet and dry years, which constitute one of the natural foundations of human life, even advanced Western nations depict a drought lasting for a few months as a disaster. Civil engineers are in the habit of gauging their dams for high-water floods, which may occur about once every thousand years, but social planners proclaim disaster when confronted by a drought which recurs as often as once or twice every hundred years.

Clearly, then, it is time that serious efforts were made by individual countries to establish sound management of their water resources. Even though the functional sectors of water supply vary from one country to another according to basic natural conditions, economic structure, and development level, the individual elements of water management remain the same: water for survival, water for plant production, water for industry, water for health services, water as a producer of energy, water as a producer of fish, and water as a basis of shipping. These elements should also include the adverse functions of water as a cause of damage, e.g., damage caused by high-water floods, water as a recipient of sewage and other effluent, the tendency of accumulations of water to attract insects which spread disease, water as a medium of infection, and the ability of a superabundance of water to cause waterlogging and to stunt the development of vegetation.

The universal nature of water problems makes it natural to pursue an interchange of experience at an international level in a bid to solve the problems of water supply now looming in our starving world. Thus, following the resolution adopted by the UN Economic and Social Committee (ECOSOC) in 1973, the UN is to hold a World Water Conference in 1977. At the invitation of Argentina, this conference will be held at Mar del Plata, Argentina, in March of that year.

First and foremost, the conference will be aimed at bringing about the improvement of preparedness at all levels— local, national, regional, and international; this is needed to prevent the development of a water crisis during the next few decades. The conference will be addressed primarily to politicians and decision makers. It will consider how the global fixed stock of water can be managed to satisfy the world's mounting need of water for domestic, agricultural, industrial, and other purposes.

Resources and needs: assessment of the world water situation

Under this heading the conference will receive a comprehensive review of water availability designed to provide an objective appraisal of the current and prospective water situation throughout the world. The availability of water will be compared with what is required to meet identified goals of availability and use. The review will include geographical characteristics and differences in levels of development, and will indicate major regional and subregional trends in the supply of and demand for water for all purposes. It will also provide the factual setting for discussions of policy options on which the work of the conference will be concentrated.

The promise of technology: potential and limitations

Apart from resources and needs, a review will be given at the water conference of the types of technological advance and of the choices of appropriate technology required to achieve, not only the greatest possible increase in the usefully available supply of water, but also improved efficiency in the use and reuse of water. Special attention will focus upon the problems of developing countries. Water-quality control requirements and pollution hazards will also be reviewed under this heading.

To be more specific, the limits to trade-offs between capital-intensive and labor-intensive techniques will be considered. Attention will be paid to the prospects of making more efficient use of local materials and to the possibilities of greater flexibility in considering the scale and size of water-resource projects. The promises of technology include techniques for achieving greater efficiency in water use, either through increased total supply or by reducing water wastage and water losses. Emphasis will also be placed on the elimination or reduction of harmful effects of water use, primarily with respect to the control and management of various types of waste water, but also in connection with floodplain management.

Furthermore, a review will be given at the conference of the possibilities of increasing water supply by the application of new techniques, such as desalinization or weather

195

modification. It should be added, however, that many present-day water scientists regard these possibilities as somewhat exaggerated. Techniques of this kind ought probably to be considered applicable at local level only.

Policy options

The reviews of resources and needs and of the promise of technology will be based on preconference work and presented in documents distributed in advance of the conference. Work during the conference itself will concentrate on a discussion of different items related to water policy and the possibilities of controlling and managing water resources so as to satisfy man's need to make positive use of water and protect himself from its negative effects. Thus, the conference will consider the ways in which water policies and institutions can best be adapted to physical, economic, social, political, and cultural conditions and examine the kinds of technology best suited to individual countries. Constraints and options of different kinds will be discussed. The types of constraints hindering the efficient development of water resources will be a prime concern here; so will capital requirements and limitations in future years, and the realistic development options open within these constraints. Manpower needs, training requirements, as well as the characteristics of institutions and laws needed to achieve efficiency in developing and using water resources are other items to be discussed. Also of central importance are water resource planning and coordination requirements, allocation criteria, and criteria for the implementation of plans and projects.

Since one of the objectives of the conference is to promote the levels of preparedness necessary to avoid a serious lack of usable water—to remedy such deficiencies as far as possible where they have already appeared and, generally, to promote better management of existing resources, it is consistent that the conference should also discuss measures to deal with water pollution. This is often a question of national concern, but it can also be an international question involving several countries when pollution that causes damage in one country derives from the discharge of pollutants in another. Pollution may be carried across national boundaries either by air masses or by transnational rivers.

Another issue of substantial international relevance, to be discussed at the conference, concerns international rivers: this is the issue of how to achieve a more efficient joint use of multinational water resources. The magnitude of this problem is clear from the fact that the majority of the world's inhabitants live in river basins whose water has to be shared by several countries, and that most of the available water resources are to be found in rivers shared between two to ten different countries.

What is to be done? Action proposals

As has been shown here, the UN World Water Conference focuses preeminently on practical action. The time available while the delegates are assembled in Mar del Plata will be devoted to as constructive an interchange of experience as possible, leading to a positive action program for the future guidance of national governments and of the many international bodies already concerned with hydrological problems.

The action program is to embrace all the national and international activities required to promote a more sensible use of global water resources. Water must be regarded as a resource which is common to the whole of humanity and which, in the course of its worldwide circulation between oceans, atmosphere, and continents, passes through each individual country and is thereby made available for use; it must not, however, be destroyed or exhausted in ways that harm other countries. Water acknowledges no national boundaries.

What are Western countries to do?

In this book we have seen a number of facts which may have

been unknown to many people. We have seen that the problem of water supply, globally speaking, is not the diminutive problem it appears to be in many well-watered countries. Formidable tasks remain to be tackled if the developing countries are to be rescued from starvation. But what can we do, living as far away as we do from the places concerned?

We have seen that these problems are of global proportions. We must not lose sight of this perspective. We must rouse ourselves to a new global awareness; we must open the window and view our own problems in relation to those which are emerging in other parts of the world. We must learn to realize that reason is today our greatest asset. Everything we do must be based on knowledge. Otherwise, our mistakes are liable to multiply so rapidly and attain such proportions that they get completely out of control.

What else can we do to help? We can train advisers specializing in the hydrological, ecological, and technological problems of the developing countries. Western countries have a tradition and reputation in international civil engineering which dates back to the closing years of the last century. For a long time now they have provided consultant services, and more recently they have developed a widespread network of international development assistance through international development authorities. At their technical colleges, elements of internationalization are being added to the training of civil engineers, planners, and community designers. The same applies to the training of hydrologists, agronomists, and forestry experts. This development must continue.

It is also important for these professional groups to learn to tackle problems on a joint basis together with ecologists, social scientists, and economists. As we have seen, hydrological questions are closely tied to social development in general and cannot be isolated from a wider context.

Thus, international assistance must be based on a sound knowledge of conditions in the countries we wish to assist. We need knowledge in order to avoid making mistakes which do more harm than good.

We can develop hydrological and ecological research to build up the necessary fund of knowledge that must be placed at the disposal of developing countries through the most varied forms of knowledge transfer. Research focusing on the developing countries must, therefore, be added to the spectrum of research activities. Due attention must be given to the problems of developing countries in postsecondary education. In fact, consideration is already being given, to internationalization of research and education along these lines.

Technically, we can also help to raise world food production by raising our own agricultural output—not least by means of improved water management.

Finally, it would be good to see the creation in industrialized countries of a political climate favoring economic generosity, with a genuine readiness to make sacrifices. Without this readiness, the economic realities of agricultural and water-resource development will pose an insuperable obstacle. It is also to be hoped that many of the adverse effects of industrialization and urbanization on the environment and on human health will act as a warning to countries in the early stages of industrialization. If developing countries could avoid repeating these principal mistakes, they would be spared a number of difficulties and troubles for which the industrialized countries have had to pay dearly— economically, in terms of water, and in human suffering.

References

Chapter 1

Johnson, D. G. *World Food Problem and Prospects: Foreign Affairs Studies.* American Enterprise Institute for Public Policy Research, Washington, D.C., 1975.

Meadows, D. H.; Meadows, D. L.; Randers, J.; and Behrens, W. W., III. *The Limits to Growth.* A Potomac Associates Book, Earth Islands, London, 1972.

Mesarovic, M., and Pestel, E. *Mankind at the Turning Point.* Second report of the Club of Rome. E.P. Dutton and Co., New York, 1974.

Poleman, T. T., and Freebairn, D. K., eds. *Food, Population and Employment: The Impact of the Green Revolution.* Praeger Publishers, New York, 1974.

UN World Food Conference, Rome 5-16 November 1974. *Assessment of the World Food Situation—Present and Future.* E/CONF 65/3; *The World Food Problem—Proposals for National and International Action.* E/CONF 65/4.

USSR. *World Water Balance and Water Resources of the Earth.* USSR National Committee for the International Hydrological Decade, Leningrad, 1974.

Chapter 2

Eriksson, E., ed. *World Water Problems—Nobel Workshop, May 1973.* International Hydrological Decade, Sweden (report no. 34). Swedish Natural Science Research Council, 1974.

Falkenmark, M., and Lindh, G. "How Can We Cope With the Water Resources Situation by the Year 2015?" *AMBIO* (Royal Swedish Academy of Sciences), no. 3-4, 1974.

Food and Agriculture Organization. *Water and the Environment.* FAO, irrigation and drainage paper no. 8, Rome, 1971.

Lowry, J. H. *World Population and Food Supply.* Edward Arnold Ltd., 1970.

Lvovich, M. I. *The World's Water.* Mir Publisher, Moscow, 1973.

Nace, R. L. *Water and Man: A World View. Unesco and Its Programme.* Unesco, 1969.

Unesco. "Human-engineering the Planet." *Impact of Science on Society.* Unesco document no. 2, 1969.

UN World Population Conference, Bucharest 19-30 August 1974. *Population Resources and the Environment.* E/CONF 60/5.

Chapter 3

Hutchinson. *Irrigation, Drainage and Salinity.* FAO and Unesco, 1970.

Lutkin, J. N. *Drainage of Agricultural Lands.* American Society of Agronomy, Madison, Wisconsin, n.d.

Winter, E. J. *Water, Soil and the Plant.* Macmillan, 1974.

Yaron, D.; Danfors, E.; and Vaadia, Y. "Arid Zone Irrigation." *Ecological Studies* 5 (Springer-Verlag), 1973.

Chapter 4

Ambroggi, R. P. "Water under the Sahara." *Scientific American* 214, no. 5, May 1966.

Eckholm, E. P. "Desertification: A World Problem." *AMBIO* (Royal Swedish Academy of Sciences) IV, no. 4, 1975.

Rapp, A. *A Review of Desertization in Africa.* Secr. for Internat. Ecology, Sweden (report no. 1), 1974.

Simons, M. *The Changing World of Deserts.* Oxford University Press, 1967.

Chapter 5

Chen Chia-chi; Yeh Yung-yi; and Tan Wei-yan. *The Impor-*

tant *Role of Historical Flood Data in the Estimation of Spillway Design Floods*. Peking, June 1974.

International Water Resources Association. *Water for the Human Environment*. Proceedings of the First World Congress on Water Resources, 1973.

Loeser, C. J. "Water Management in China." *Water Resources Bulletin* 9, no. 1, February 1973.

Chapter 6

Lisoni, L., and Stretta, E. *Hydrological Studies of the Upper Paraguay River Basin (Pantanel Region, Mato Grosso State, Brazil): Nature and Resources*. Unesco, Paris, 1973.

Unesco. *Brazil, Hydrological Studies of the Upper Paraguay River Basin (Pantanel), 1966-72*. Technical report, 1973.

Chapter 7

Howe, Ch. W., and Easter, K. W. *Interbasin Transfers of Water*. The Johns Hopkins Press, 1971.

McPherson, M. B., ed. *Hydrological Effects of Urbanization*. The Unesco Press, Paris, 1974.

Szesztay, K. *The Hydrosphere and the Human Environments. Results of Research on Representative and Experimental Basins (Wellington Symposium 1970)*. International Association on Scientific Hydrology, Paris, 1973.

Chapter 8

Eriksson, E., ed. *World Water Problems—Nobel Workshop, May 1973*. International Hydrological Decade, Sweden (report no. 34). Swedish Natural Science Research Council, 1974.

Wiener, A. *The Role of Water in Development*. McGraw-Hill, New York, 1972.

Chapter 9

Anderla, G. *Information in 1985.* OECD, Paris, 1973.

Boutry, G-A. "Quantity Versus Quality in Scientific Research." *Impact of Science on Society* XX, no. 3, Unesco, Paris, 1973.

Vlachos, E., ed. *Transfer of Water Resources Knowledge.* Proceedings of the First International Conference on Transfer of Water Resources Knowledge. Water Resources Publications, Fort Collins, Colorado, 1973.

Chapter 10

Biswas, A. K. *History of Hydrology.* North Holland Publishing, 1970.

Doxiadis, C. A. *Global Action for Man's Water Resources: Water for the Human Environment.* International Water Resources Association, First World Congress, Chicago, 1973.

Food and Agriculture Organization. *Man's Influence on the Hydrological Cycle.* FAO, irrigation and drainage paper no. 17, Rome, 1973.